KISSING THE TRAIL

KISSING THE TRAIL

GREATER SEATTLE MOUNTAIN BIKE ADVENTURES

• THIRD EDITION •

John Zilly

ADVENTURE PRESS

SEATTLE, WASHINGTON

Kissing the Trail: Greater Seattle Mountain Bike Adventures, Third Edition
© 2003 by John Zilly

Copyeditor: Emily Bedard
Cover and interior design: Peter D'Agostino
Cover photo: Colin Meagher (Rider: Angela Sucich on Dalles Ridge, see Rides 47, 48)
Interior photos:
    Angela Castañeda, Colin Meagher, Wade Praeger, Greg Strong, John Zilly, Peter Zilly
    Photo on page 22 courtesy of the Special Collections Division,
        University of Washington Libraries, photo by Wilse, #835.5.
    Photo on page 23 courtesy of the Museum of History & Industry (2,968)
    Photo on page 31 courtesy of the Museum of History & Industry (13,467)
Maps: John Zilly

ISBN: 1-881583-09-0

Adventure Press
P.O. Box 14059
Seattle, Washington 98114
206-200-2578 (v), 206-568-0592 (f)

MANY THANKS

Marea Angela Castañeda helped me tremendously on *Kissing the Trail* with ideas, assistance, and constant encouragement. I fell in love with her while I wrote it. She is my First Kiss.

Steve Hall was the catalyst to get this project rolling, so to speak. His ideas always proved useful, and even with this third edition it's difficult to imagine this book without his help.

This third edition could not have been completed in a timely way without the enormous help of Tom Zilly and Jane Noland. Thank you, thank you, thank you.

For their assistance and contributions, thanks to David Baldwin, Mike Clyde, Peter D'Agostino, Steve DeBroux, David Graves, Mark Klebanoff, Bob Rohan, Greg Strong, Fred Wert, Lisa Dally Wilson, Fred Wilson, Paul Zilly, and Peter Zilly.

And for all standing around in the rain, thanks to my riding partners.

OVERVIEW MAP

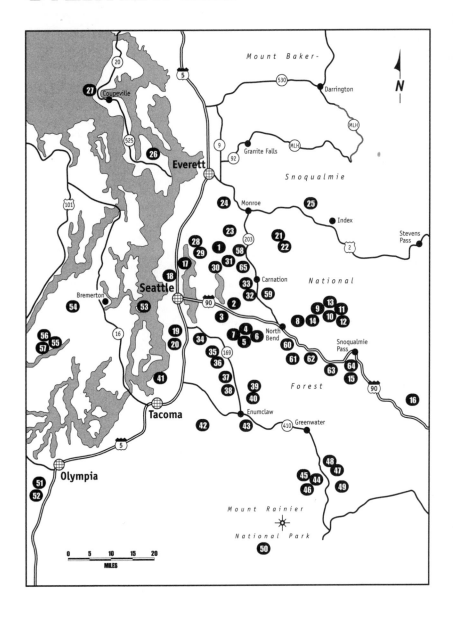

CONTENTS

CONTENTS

RIDES BY DIFFICULTY

EASY ✹

Ride#	Ride Name	Best Season	Kids	Fee
18	Lower Woodland Park	spring summer fall winter	kids!	
36	Lake Wilderness	spring summer fall winter	kids!	
40	Nolte State Park	spring summer fall	kids!	yes
58	Duvall to Carnation	spring summer fall winter	kids!	
60	Boxley Creek	spring summer fall winter	kids!	
64	Iron Horse State Park: Snoqualmie Tunnel	summer fall	kids!	yes

INTERMEDIATE ✹ ✹

Ride#	Ride Name	Best Season	Kids	Fee
12	Goldmyer Hotsprings	summer fall		yes
17	Hamlin Park	spring summer fall winter	kids!	
19	North Seatac Park	spring summer fall winter	kids!	
21	Drunken Charlie Lake	spring summer fall winter		
22	Marckworth Forest	spring summer fall winter		
28	Saint Edward State Park	spring summer fall	kids!	yes
31	Redmond Watershed	spring summer fall	kids!	
35	Lake Youngs	spring summer fall winter	kids!	
50	Westside Road	summer fall		yes
53	Blake Island State Park	spring summer fall winter	kids!	
59	Snoqualmie Valley Trail	spring summer fall winter	kids!	
61	Iron Horse State Park: Rattlesnake Lake	spring summer fall winter	kids!	yes

DIFFICULT ✹ ✹ ✹

Ride#	Ride Name	Best Season	Kids	Fee
2	Grand Ridge	spring summer fall winter		
3	Issaquah to Grand Ridge	spring summer fall winter		
5	Iverson Railroad Grade	spring summer fall		
6	Crossover Road	spring summer fall winter		
8	CCC Road	spring summer fall		
9	CCC Extension	summer fall		yes
10	Middle Fork of the Snoqualmie River	summer fall		yes

RIDES BY DIFFICULTY

DIFFICULT ✸ ✸ ✸

Ride#	Ride Name	Best Season	Kids	Fee
13	Taylor River	summer fall		yes
20	South Seatac Park	spring summer fall winter		
23	Paradise Valley	spring summer fall winter		
24	Lord Hill Park	spring summer fall winter		
25	Wallace Falls State Park	spring summer fall		yes
26	Goss Lake Woods	spring summer fall winter		
27	Fort Ebey State Park	spring summer fall winter		yes
29	Big Finn Hill	spring summer fall		yes
30	Sammamish River Rambler	spring summer fall winter		yes
32	Tolt-MacDonald North	spring summer fall winter		
33	Tolt-MacDonald South	spring summer fall winter		
34	Tapeworm	spring summer fall winter		
37	The Woods	spring summer fall		
38	Black Diamond Lake	spring summer fall winter		
39	Kanaskat-Palmer	spring summer fall	kids!	yes
41	Dash Point State Park	summer fall	kids!	yes
42	Victor Falls	spring summer fall winter		
43	Mud Mountain	spring summer fall winter	kids!	
46	Fawn Ridge	summer fall		yes
54	Green Mountain	spring summer fall winter		
55	Northwest Passage	spring summer fall winter		
57	Howell Lake	spring summer fall winter		
62	Iron Horse State Park: Humpback Mountain	spring summer fall		yes
63	Iron Horse State Park: Keechelus Lake	summer fall		yes

MOST DIFFICULT ✸ ✸ ✸ ✸

Ride#	Ride Name	Best Season	Kids	Fee
4	Preston Railroad Grade	spring summer fall		
7	Poo Poo Point	spring summer fall winter		
11	Middle Fork—Extended	summer fall		yes
15	Windy Pass	summer fall		

RIDES BY DIFFICULTY

MOST DIFFICULT ✾✾✾✾

Ride#	Ride Name	Best Season	Kids	Fee
16	Kachess Ridge	summer fall		yes
44	Skookum Flats	summer fall		yes
45	Sun Top	summer fall		yes
48	Ranger Creek	summer fall		yes
49	Crystal Mountain	summer fall		
51	Porter Creek	summer fall		
52	Mima Creek	spring summer fall		
56	Stimson Creek	spring summer fall winter		

EXTREME EPIC ✾✾✾✾✾

Ride#	Ride Name	Best Season	Kids	Fee
1	The Last Dirt Trail: RIP	spring summer fall winter		
14	Middle Fork Grand Tour	summer		
47	Palisades Trail	summer fall		yes
65	Grand Railroad Tour	summer fall		

BE RESPONSIBLE

The author and publisher of *Kissing the Trail* disclaim and are in no way responsible or liable for the consequences of using this guide. Mountain biking is dangerous. Cyclists can get lost, become injured, or suffer from serious fatigue. The difficulty and skill ratings in this guide are subjective. It is incumbent on each rider to assess his or her preparedness for a trail in light of his or her own skills, experience, and equipment. The information contained in this book, is as accurate as possible, but trail conditions change without notice, for all sorts of reasons, in some cases making them dangerous or even unridable.

Do not ride on any private property unless you are sure the landowner has granted permission. Do not conclude that the owner has granted you permission to use the trails listed in this book. If you are not sure of a trail's status, you should obtain permission from the owner before riding on the property. Most of the rides described in this guide are located on public land. Although these are currently legal rides, land managers may regulate bicycle use in the future. Understanding the laws as they change is up to you.

The author assumes absolutely no responsibility for these or any other problems that may occur, nor should he. Hey kids, have fun, but be responsible for yourselves.

PREFACE TO THIRD EDITION

Woof! Since the last edition, I've written *Mountain Bike! Northwest Washington, Mountain Bike! Southwest Washington, Kissing the Trail: Northwest and Central Oregon,* and *Beyond Mount Si: The Best Hikes within 85 Miles of Seattle.* I'm happy to say there are a lot of great trails out there. But last year when I took a look at *Kissing the Trail: Greater Seattle Mountain Bike Adventures,* I found it was in serious need of cables, a bottom bracket, and some new titanium parts. And that's what's here.

What's bad: First, urban sprawl has chewed away at even more trails; I could put together a thick book of trails that have been discarded since the first edition of *Kissing the Trail* was published in 1993. Bummer, because nearby open space is one of the things that keeps us sane in an otherwise crazy world. Second, the trails at Tiger Mountain are still closed for half the year—and they shouldn't be. Third, when the second edition of *Kissing the Trail* came out, the Forest Service was working on a plan for the Middle Fork of the Snoqualmie River Trail. Well, they're still working on it. The trail will likely re-open to bikes in 2003 on an every-other-day basis, but that is not certain. I've included a few rides that traverse this trail, but we'll have to wait until the Middle Fork plan is finalized before we can ride there.

What's good: New places to ride. In the 1990s, mountain bikers got off on exploring grimy doubletracks to who-knows-where. Today, twisty user-built singletrack is the thing. Check out the new trails at Tolt-MacDonald Park, Paradise Valley, Goss Lake Woods, Victor Falls, Black Diamond Lake, and The Woods— just a few of the 18 new rides in this edition. All of the other information has, of course, been tuned, polished, and updated. Now it's time to go give the trails a kiss.

John Zilly
February 2003

BE COOL TO THE EARTH

Some people contend that revealing these wonderful rides will surely ruin them. To someone who loves the solitude and majesty of special places, it is certainly a dilemma. Why would I want more people out on the trails I love, more people intruding on my peace, diminishing my experience? Surely I shouldn't tell more people about these great adventures.

But this don't-tell-anyone attitude represents short-range thinking. I want to hike the Pacific Crest Trail when I'm seventy. When I asked a friend to plan on the trip, some forty years in the future, he said, "There won't be a Pacific Crest Trail when we're seventy." He could be right: economic and social pressures have greatly reduced trail mileage in this country over the past twenty years. We are losing trails because not enough people are willing to fight for them, to work on them, and to pay for them. Most folks don't appreciate public lands until they have spent some time in them, felt their beauty and power. True, sending more people out onto trails causes a greater impact, but it's also true that more people will learn to love the land that, perhaps, shouldn't be mined or clearcut. To preserve trails—especially those close to urban centers—more people, not fewer, need to know and love them. If more people enjoy beautiful trails, then more voices will be able to shout when development or logging or governmental cutbacks threaten to eliminate them.

I am a conservationist, committed to preserving the public lands we all own. But I am a conservationist who rides a mountain bicycle. Unfortunately, due to a few renegades, mountain bicyclists have a rather bad reputation vis-à-vis the environment, a reputation we don't deserve. And now 90 percent of the trails in King County have been closed to mountain bikes. This short-sighted action by other user groups and trail bureaucrats will actually decrease and degrade the number of trails and primitive areas rather than increase and enhance them. That's because these groups are spurning a huge pool of conservationists—mountain bicyclists—who also want to preserve and, indeed, increase the number of primitive areas. Bicyclists have always been part of the conservation movement, and mountain bikers are no different. Mountain bicyclists don't demand paved trails, which are expensive and degrade the land's beauty. Mountain bicyclists usually don't camp overnight on the land that they use, reducing that impact. Mountain bicyclists can sometimes ride to the trailhead, so cars are driven less and there's no need for more parking lots. And mountain bicyclists are generally cycling enthusiasts who commute to work, ride for groceries, and pedal for their "Sunday drive."

If all goes well, if we pedal into primitive areas to enjoy the land and if we also help to preserve it, perhaps there will be a Pacific Crest Trail to hike in the year 2030.

THE FIRST KISS

When was your first kiss? Steady yourself and think back for a moment. My first kiss took place one summer afternoon on top of a dog house. It had been planned for several days; the locale was carefully chosen for its secluded nature, although in retrospect the choice seems more like a podium than a secret kissing alcove. Since the dog house was taller than either of us, Tina and I helped each other climb to the crest. Moments later the first kiss ensued. Bliss. The kissman, kiss-o-rama, kisselodeon, osculating on the dog house, winning the Oscar, making a speech, kiss-tosterone, kissapalooza, kiss-o-mania, k-i-s-s. Since then the moment has tirelessly wandered the back alleys of my memory, exposing itself to my consciousness every so often. It makes me laugh; it makes me smile. The memory says to me, "Don't be so serious, or safe, or sure of the way things should proceed." Sometimes it's the proceeding that's important. Shouldn't there be more moments like this that flow through your mind's hot-water pipes? When is the next event that will resonate with first-kiss magnitude? How long has it been?

Pump up the tires and hold on tight. For this, trust one Neil Cassidy, an iconoclast of the Beat Generation, friend of Kerouac, Kesey, and the Grateful Dead. Cassidy lived a fervid, shortish life, driving cartwheel-colored buses, borrowed cars, and possibly owned Cadillacs all over the Americas, always searching. The nectar is in the journey, he may have said. In a song about Neil Cassidy, John Barlow writes, "Ah, child of boundless trees. Ah, child of boundless seas. What you are, what you're meant to be . . . " And later, Cassidy is "lost now on these country miles in his Cadillac." Whenever I hear these lines, I have strong urges to unloose my child of boundless dreams and hit the road or—even better—the trail.

While this doesn't necessarily mean that we all ought to file into the boss's office and quit, it does mean we need to be spirited and enthusiastic, get a grip on reality. Over the past 30 years, Americans have dispensed with about half of their free time. Between commuting, longer work hours, and multi-career families, we don't have much free time left. The average person (car, job, kid, and basement that resembles a landfill) has just 16 hours of free time a week after brushing his teeth and shoveling in that microwaved entrée. It has become a monumental task to scrounge enough time for a weekend outing, let alone a drive across America. Time for a First Kiss? Hardly. But we can use the time we do have in a passionate and adventurous manner, rather than a tepid and guarded one. With that in mind, it's time to get out and be passionate about the outdoors. It's time for some mountain biking. *Kissing the Trail* serves up 65 great mountain bike rides for all abilities, all within 85 miles of Seattle. No other mountain bike guide points the way to so many rides so close to home on good, soft-surface, public *and* private trails. Charging out to experience life with First Kiss passion is still possible; you just have to choose it. But mountain

bicycling involves a lot more than finding the trailhead and knowing when to turn left. So I have also included sections on safety, riding techniques, repairs, training, maintenance, land issues, and ethics.

Here are my goals for this book: To inform families, weekend cyclists, and mountain-bike fanatics about great trails; to encourage them to ride in a safe and intelligent way; to spread out mountain bicyclists onto lots of trails; to show that users can share trails without conflict; and to remind people of something they already know—that bicyclists really are part of the conservation movement.

Kissing the Trail is about mountain biking with an attitude, holding on to boundless dreams, mediating the stresses, but it's also about being safe and considerate and conservation-minded while out on the trail. It is possible to have a serious craving for a First Kiss experience and still pay attention to where you are and how you got there, to care for the few giant cedars left in the forest, and to be courteous to others using the same trail. More preaching, prophesying, and playing to come, so open an unknown door, skip off to see the wizard, cop a lost-now-on-a-country-road-in-a-Cadillac feel (even if the p.c. rating of a 1960s-era Caddy is, well, tank empty).

USING THIS GUIDE

Whether you began mountain biking yesterday or have been racing for years, this trail guide is exactly what you need to explore the trails around Puget Sound. Despite the setback of numerous trail closures, many miles of public and private "community" trails still exist in the Puget Sound region.

The straightforward format of *Kissing the Trail* makes it easy to select the type of ride you are looking for. Rides which begin from the same trailhead are treated as two separate rides, so the confusing exercise of skipping every other paragraph or map is eliminated. Here's a rundown of the information provided with each ride, from the wheel rating and ride statistics to the maps and ride description.

Difficulty Rating

The difficulty rating is measured from **1 to 5 wheels**, depending on the length of the trip, the hill factor, and the level of riding skill required. This quick reference is located at the top of each ride.

Easy: Just about anyone can ride a one-wheel ride; it isn't much different from riding on a paved country road. These rides are generally short and not very hilly, with a well-packed riding surface. One-wheel rides stick to wide, nontechnical dirt roads or easy rail-trails.

Intermediate: A two-wheel ride usually follows dirt roads and rail-trails, but it can wander onto jeep roads and singletrack. These rides are longer and may have more elevation gain than one-wheelers. The riding, however, isn't technical.

Difficult: During a three-wheel ride you may encounter dirt roads, but you will certainly experience singletrack trails. These rides are longer, have some steep climbs, and cross tricky spots in the trail that will likely require walking your bike, perhaps over some longer sections.

Most Difficult: If a ride is long, hilly, and full of technical riding, I have rated it four wheels. Some riders may have to push or carry their bikes for long stretches. Remember: If you're not hiking, you're not mountain biking.

 **Extreme Epic:** Whoa! Several rides are sufficiently difficult to warrant a five-wheel rating. These rides are very long, technical, hilly, and even dangerous. Don't attempt them unless you are an expert in great physical condition.

Ride Statistics

Distance: Trip distance is listed at the top of each ride. Remember: One mile on a dirt trail equals three to five on a road. Each ride is labeled **out and back**, **loop**, **lollipop loop**, or **one way**.

Terrain: Here's a snapshot of the ride—singletrack or dirt road, steep climb or pancake flat. Cumulative elevation gains are listed.

Duration: The duration of each ride is only approximate, since this ultimately depends on the rider's skill, stamina, and map-reading abilities. Also, a ride that takes one hour in July could take five in January if it's muddy or there is a lot of blowdown.

Travel: Lists how far the trailhead is from Seattle.

Skill Level: Rides are rated **beginner**, **intermediate**, **advanced**, or **expert** depending on the minimum bike-handling ability a rider should have before attempting a particular trail.

Season: Best time of year and seasonal trail closures are noted.

Maps: Supplementary maps are key, unless you like bivouacking. They are typically United States Geological Survey (USGS), Green Trails, or Washington State Forest maps.

Explorability: Listed as **low**, **moderate**, or **high**, this rating reveals the presence (or lack) of other trails or roads in the vicinity that may not be on the map. Have fun, but don't get too lost.

Restrictions: Lists the rules, regulations, restrictions, and fees.

More Info: Pertinent phone numbers and websites.

Prelude

Each ride begins with a paragraph that presents a general sense of the ride. Magic is performed here, and ride karma is released.

Driving Directions

Locating the starting point of each ride is simple—just follow these concise directions to the trailhead.

The Ride

This section contains a detailed description of the terrain—up or down, left or right. These paragraphs note the **mileage**, in bold, for most intersections, hills, and other significant landmarks. By the way, riding with an odometer is highly recommended. Here are a few of the conventions I use while describing the rides: **Whoa** signifies a dangerous section of trail or a turn easily missed, and warns the rider to pay close attention. **Woof!** indicates the crest of a particularly tough hill. **Stay on the main trail/road** means that other trails may exit from the main trail—use good judgment to remain on the obvious main line. When the trail deadends at another trail, forcing a 90-degree turn either right or left, the resulting three-way intersection is described as a **T**. Other three-way intersections are described as **forks** or **the trail divides**. When two trails cross, the result is usually referred to as a **4-way intersection**.

There are a number of different types of trails described in this book. A **dirt or gravel road** could be used by a car. **Jeep trails**, sometimes known as **doubletracks**, refer to rough roads that only jeep-type vehicles could navigate. Old **railroad grades**, or **rail-trails**, are abandoned railroad lines that have no tracks or ties. Typically, rail-trails have the look and feel of dirt roads, with the exception that rail-trails almost always seem flat. **Trails** and **singletrack**, used interchangeably, generally refer to soft-surface trails less than 48 inches wide, though "trail" is also used in a generic sense. **Hiking-only trails** mean stay off. **Paved trails**, often rail-trails, and paved roads are noted as such.

Notes

Here's where you get to start writing your own guidebook, or at least your mountain bike diary.

THE MAPS

What can I say here? Just about every ride has one. The maps are informative and easy to use. The highlighted route, micro legend, and elevation markers are a few of the handy features. I tried to make them full of information specifically pertinent to mountain bikers. I created the maps using USGS maps, data from a GPS recorder (thus GPS mapping), and an altimeter, so they are accurate as well as easy to use.

OTHER DESTINATIONS

Several rides in *Kissing the Trail* fall into the Other Destinations category. What are those? Other Destinations are small areas with a maze of trails open to mountain bikes. Lots of people ride at these places; everyone has their own route, and the routes usually double-back on each other numerous times. South Seatac Park is a perfect example—it's not a big area, yet there are lots of trails. In fact, there are trails everywhere. If I drew a map and wrote up a route for South Seatac Park, you'd be reading the route description for more time than you'd be actually riding. So, instead, I've included driving directions and a short general overview, but no map or detailed route description. Have fun figuring out your own route.

Bike abandoned in search of Other Destinations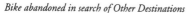

SAFETY CONCERNS

I felt a tremendous rush at age seven when I rode a bicycle without training wheels for the first time. (A little like a first kiss, in fact.) A component of the excitement was the realization that I had discovered something very dangerous. It never quite made sense to me that my parents encouraged me to go riding as much as they did. "If you go near that construction site, you'll be grounded for a month! Why don't you go out and ride your bike instead?" Okay, so I'm not supposed to dig in the dirt around an unfinished building, but riding around the neighborhood is perfectly safe? I don't think so. Though it never got me into trouble with my folks, riding down dirt embankments, sailing off plywood jumps, avoiding stray vehicles, escaping vicious dogs, and dodging neighborhood bullies wasn't exactly safe.

And I still get wide-eyed on certain trails: Mountain biking can be dangerous. Some even argue that you aren't pushing the envelope enough if you don't crash once in a while. Me? I try to avoid the cartwheeling endo. The main thing is to ride at a moderate speed and in a controlled manner. Stay away from trails above your ability. Of course at some point a fall is inevitable. To minimize the effects of a bad crash, always wear a helmet, carry a first-aid kit, and ride with a friend who can scurry off for help. But the danger of mountain biking isn't just the big crash. A simple mechanical failure, a sore knee, or exhaustion can strand you miles from the trailhead and force an unplanned night in the woods. If you don't have proper supplies like food, extra clothes, enough water, a light, and a stick to fend off the wild pigs, you are in trouble. Everyone defines danger and adventure differently: Just try to turn around before your adventure turns into a nightmare.

Minimize Risks

- Never ride alone.
- Always wear a helmet.
- Avoid violent speed experiences and out-of-control riding. Watch out for other trail users, ruts, roots, rocks, fallen trees, cliffs, and all animals.
- Carry a good first-aid kit and know how to use it. Also toss sunscreen, a lighter, a pocket knife, some food, and a flashlight into that fanny pack.
- Wear eye protection.
- Take two quarts of water per person per day. Don't count on finding water.
- Always, always, always take along a good map, a compass, and an odometer.
- Carry extra clothes no matter how nice the weather seems.
- Make sure someone in the group has the proper bike-repair tools.
- Is it hunting season? Wear a bell and something bright, or go road riding. A bullet hole in your new jersey is a sure way to ruin the ride.

VIRTUOUS MOUNTAIN BIKING

You're out on the trail, admiring an enormous cedar, listening to the river below. You're having quite a bit more fun than you do at work, at least a thousand times the fun. This is not, however, the time to disconnect your intuition about good and bad; it's time to listen to your heart and ask, "How do I go out into a primitive area on a bike and act virtuously? What's the point of being out here anyway?"

Well, there needs to be magic and wonder. Stop to watch a deer in the meadow, a hawk, a spirited stream empowered by snow melt; see a chipmunk chipmunking instead of a co-worker bitching; discover the smell of a pine forest instead of the electrified-defrosted-conditioned-reconstituted-smogged-exhausted air of the city. It's true, there is a roller-coaster element to mountain biking. The adventure involves speed, technical riding skills, a modicum of danger, and buckets of physicality. But mere physicality does not equal adventure; adventure contains romance and magic. If you are not after this magic, if all that interests you is raging down one hill after another, stay home and turn on the television; you are not wanted on the trail.

Fortunately, the speed freaks and havoc-wreakers represent a small minority of the mountain bike community, just as hikers who cut switchbacks are a minority in that community. Most riders do search out the magic that's hidden around each bend in the trail. These are the ones who always yield the trail to others and help maintain trails. These are virtuous mountain bicyclists. But it's not quite that easy. Mountain bicyclists have been made pariahs of the forest, banned here, restricted there. What follows is a discussion of the issues, and non-issues, that have brought mountain bicyclists to this point.

The Lake Washington Bicycle Path, circa 1900

Safety

Earlier I said that mountain bikers can be terrors to themselves—flying off cliffs and launching into large trees. Now, discussing ethics, I need to explain the concept of public safety. Only your mom may care if you fly off the edge of a canyon, but when you careen around a corner and run down small children, many people care. And they don't like you as much as your mom. But virtuous riding is not really about who gets upset. The virtuous rider does not run anyone down simply because it's not right.

The safety problem arises because mountain bikers are quiet and can sometimes travel more quickly than pedestrians. On downhills, cyclists can come up on other users quickly. To alleviate a mishap, ride

Mountain bicycle pioneers in Seattle, circa 1900

as if a small child is around every corner. Attach a bell to your bike to alert other trail users of your presence. Trail users simply need to be considerate of each other. If you are out on the trail, yield to all trail users, whether hikers, equestrians, motorcyclists, or other bicyclists.

The United States Forest Service has banned mountain bicycles from many trails. The Snoqualmie Ranger District's North Bend region, for instance, permits mountain bicycles on just a few trails. At most trailheads, though, signs pronounce the trail closed due to user conflict. Since I haven't seen users fist-fighting, I assume the rangers are concerned about the safety of the different types of users on the same trail. I biked several thousand miles during the research for *Kissing the Trail*, and I never had a conflict with another trail user. Moreover, I've never had a conflict while researching any of the ten guidebooks I've written. Just because the uses are different does not mean they are incompatible.

The Environment

Everyone who enters a primitive area should take responsibility for minimizing his or her impact. Although "no-trace use" is the code of the day, all travelers have an impact on the environment—even if it's a turned pine cone or a lingering odor. An average mountain bike weighs about 25 pounds, less than a full backpack, so a loaded hiker bounding down the trail weighs more than a mountain bicyclist (equestrians, on the other hand, are off the scale). True, trail damage based on weight doesn't tell the entire tale, but scientific studies have proven that on dry, well-built trails, Vibram-footed hikers and rolling wheels have about the same impact. On poorly constructed trails and on all trails during bad weather, all users cause damage. It's up to each user—hiker, equestrian, cyclist—to survey the impact and take steps to prevent damage—even if it means turning around and heading home.

Some areas are very susceptible to damage, and you should ride these with care. Other areas have been crisscrossed by four-wheel drives, backhoes, and logging equipment—go ahead and get muddy on these. Both sorts of trails are included here, just make sure to be nice to the trails that need it. Check out each trail carefully, then use good sense to determine whether it ought to be ridden.

There is one specific type of damage that mountain bikes do have an exclusive claim to—tire impressions. These are created by the skidding action of beginning cyclists. Mountain bikers should learn how to ride to prevent skidding (unless on pavement or gravel). Simply riding on a particularly delicate trail can cause damage—a slight dent can form which might cause erosion during a hard rain. To prevent this, always watch the trail for signs of damage. Trail conditions can change quickly, so one section of a ride might be fine while the next section should not be used. Turn around if you are causing damage.

The greatest damage to trails and the environment comes not from wheels or boots but from simple overuse. The Alpine Lakes Wilderness, near Snoqualmie Pass, has been heavily damaged by the million hikers and equestrians each year who enter its boundaries. The key is to act virtuously *and* spread out the use. Over the past twenty years, the number of miles of trails in the United States has actually decreased while the population has continued its steady climb: More people are traversing fewer trails. There is a need for more trails—on primitive and semi-primitive land close to urban areas—that are open to all users. Open trail policies combined with maps and other resources like *Kissing the Trail* will help disperse trail use and thus minimize the most serious environmental impact—overcrowding.

Aesthetics

Hiking groups have been exceptionally vocal in their opposition to mountain bikes. But it's an aesthetic problem, not a trail-use problem: User conflict and environmental damage are euphemisms for a not-on-my-trail attitude held by a few flannel-shirted bullies. Of course, these dull, mingy-minded thinkers have been around for a long time. In an 1882 article for *The Wheelman* about mountain biking in the Rocky Mountains, the writer W.O. Owen wrote that he met a "big, burly fellow" in La Porte, Colorado, who called Owen's bicycle "some infernal machine, or Yankee contrivance." Sound familiar?

Mountain bicycles have been known to offend the sensibilities of such hikers, who hike in to a lake, set up camp, and don't want to see any foam-helmeted cyclist roll up at 10 a.m. I understand. It's not the bike or the helmet that's the problem, however; it's the feeling that another person is infringing on your space. When I go mountain biking, I don't want to see zillions of people. If I do, I might select a different trail the next time. And if I spend five hours hiking up to a secluded lake, I'm disappointed if confronted with a set of yellow tent domes. Most trail users venture into primitive areas to get away from the crowds, to be self-sufficient, to be out there, not to be accosted by other humans. The sight of unprepared trail users panhandling for water and granola bars on a hot day is not why we head out into the woods.

Some have argued, spuriously of course, that mountain bicycles are a new use, and thus upset the proprietary grip hikers and equestrians hold on public lands; others just say mountain bicyclists are environmentally bankrupt. But while the term "mountain bicycle" is relatively new, hearty cyclists have been experiencing the beauty and wonder of remote areas on bicycles for over a century. In an article describing a bicycle tour from Laramie to Cheyenne, Wyoming, in an 1883 issue of *The Wheelman*, W.O. Owen writes: "All around us beautiful evergreens tossed in the wind, each one gorgeously attired in Nature's own drapery; frost sparkling brilliantly in the sun's rays and dazing the eye with its silvery scintillation." Owen was out there for the same reason most mountain bikers are—for the wonderful experience of biking through Nature.

A ride through Nature

The Dispute

Despite the reasonable nature of mountain bikers, many areas have been closed to us. The problem? The dispute over rights. Currently, mountain bikes are excluded from trails in all national parks and completely barred from all designated Wilderness areas. In addition, many local jurisdictions have restricted the use of mountain bikes. Around Puget Sound, bicycles are banned on trails in Mount Rainier National Park, the Alpine Lakes Wilderness, most trails in the Snoqualmie–Mount Baker National Forest, the Pacific Crest Trail, all of Cougar and Squak Mountains, much of Tiger Mountain, and Seattle city parks, to name a few places.

Mountain bicycles are banned even though thousands of miles of perfectly suited trails exist. For instance, Cougar and Tiger mountains, two large, semi-primitive mountains in the Issaquah Alps, were almost completely denuded early this century. Many miles of old railroad grades, forgotten utility roads, and abandoned logging roads, hidden by second-growth forests, crisscross the two mountains. Pedestrians use some of these routes frequently, others rarely or not at all. Yet, mountain bikes are banned. Why?

During the recent mountain bicycle boom, land managers didn't have a column in their manuals for mountain bicycles. Egged on by a small number of belligerent hikers, the managers penned in mountain bikes next to motorcycles. But bicycles are fundamentally different from motorcycles; when motors hit mud, noise explodes through the forest, exhaust boils up around the flora, and pieces of trail splatter in all directions. The virtuous mountain biker tiptoes across delicate areas; motorcyclists don't sling their machines over their shoulders and tiptoe anywhere.

To make matters worse, grandfather rights have allowed the continued access of horses and miners, both egregious environmental offenders, into Wilderness areas—the most pristine lands we have. Miners cause more damage on public lands than all other users combined. They build roads up unstable hillsides, dig huge holes in the earth, throw dangerous tailings all over the place, and drag in all manner of equipment to help them. Horses, nearly as bad, dig up the flora, stomp right through delicate spots, and sometimes eradicate hillside trails. Low-impact adventuring dictates that you bury your pucky a hundred yards from any water and pack out the used paper; horses are allowed to deposit bushel loads in the middle of the trail. Give me a break.

Users need to make personal decisions about the way they interact with the woods. If the way you interact with public land adversely affects me, then either you shouldn't be doing it, or you should pay me for the inconvenience. When trail users damage sensitive areas—and there can be no argument that motorcyclists, equestrians, and miners do—they should pay the rest of us for damaging our land, through restrictions or taxes or user fees based on real, science-based impact. Mountain bikers could pay these fees too, as long as we have trails to ride. To further the cause, you can help educate land managers, legislators, and the media about mountain bicycling (see page 39). Tell them which trails you enjoy, which closed trails you would like to enjoy, and then tell them you are a bicyclist *and* an environmentalist. It's not a contradiction in terms.

Green Mountain Biking

Cyclists have been a central part of the conservation movement for years—commuting, vacationing, running errands on bicycles. And bicyclists have been building and sharing soft-surface trails around Puget Sound for over 100 years. Just check out the series of historical mountain bike photos in this introduction. Today, most mountain bicyclists call themselves "environmentalists." Here are some of the ways in which mountain bicyclists have continued this tradition of "green" living. **One:** Mountain bicycles spread out trail use so that each area receives less impact. **Two:** Mountain biking motivates more people to get out to areas that should be preserved. **Three:** Mountain bicyclists generally don't spend the night in the woods, eliminating that impact. **Four:** Mountain bikers can sometimes pedal to the trailhead rather than driving, cutting emissions and the need for paved parking areas. **Five:** Mountain bicyclists don't want paved trails, a costly degradation of the land. **Six:** Because they've been pushed out of the nice areas, mountain bikers often ride in areas that have been used as refrigerator dumps, kegger sites, and recreational

Geese at Rattlesnake Lake

shooting ranges. In these areas, expanded trail use keeps the less desirable uses away.

The bicycle industry now sells nontoxic chain lube, non-toxic citrus-based degreaser, and lights built to use rechargeable batteries. Ask for these items at the bike shop you frequent. Finally, eat organically and low on the food chain—the whole world is overcrowded, not just your favorite primitive trail.

The Rules

- Don't leave any trace: That means no Power Bar wrappers, no treadmarks on delicate trails, no toilet paper, no cigarette butts, and no clear plastic strips from the back of inner-tube patches. Pick up litter whenever possible.
- Don't skid—ever. Don't ride on poorly made trails, wet trails, or areas where the earth is liable to be marred by tires. Walk around all delicate areas.
- Respect all other trail users. Yield the right of way to everyone, including hikers, runners, other bicyclists, motorcycles, and horses.
- Stop and dismount when you encounter horses. Stand on the downhill side of the trail, and talk to the horse and rider as they pass.
- Ride in control. For your safety and others, master low-speed riding.
- Respect wildlife (you are in their home!) and livestock.
- Join an environmental group and tell them how cool mountain bikers are.
- Never come screaming around blind corners at fifty miles per hour screaming "Behold a mountain biker from hell!"

WHOSE LAND IS *THIS?*

Most of the rides in *Kissing the Trail* are on public land. But some rides use informal community trails on private land. The trails in this book that do cross private land have a long history of community use. Some landowners have posted signs that allow non-intrusive, daytime use by bicyclists and other users; other owners allow cyclists to use the land but haven't gone to the trouble of putting up signs. But owners can be fickle—allowing use one day, tacking up No Trespassing signs the next. If the property is not signed, or you are not sure of its status, you should probably get permission from the owner before riding there. Obviously, when faced with No Trespassing signs—especially the tin version pounded by bullets—it's prudent to find another ride. The author does not condone or encourage trespassing onto private property. *Kissing the Trail* simply points out areas where bicyclists, equestrians, and pedestrians have spent time over the years, usually because these areas are beautiful and close to Seattle.

Time to turn around

As of winter 2003, none of these trails cross through anyone's front yard. However, much of the private land mentioned in this book will be developed within the next ten years, some of it over the next two. Given this, a ride that doesn't cross any front yards in 2003 might well do so in 2005. The incentive for mountain bicyclists is huge: Enjoy these areas now, for they may soon be covered by evil cement. When the devil development comes—and it can happen quickly—it's time to go ride somewhere else.

Trails that have been used over the years by the community for low-impact recreation should be preserved, whether the property is public or private. If trails exist in an area scheduled to be developed, the public should demand that developers preserve those trails before the digging begins. When public jurisdictions acquire open space (as they should), issue use permits, or implement regional plans, trails should be kept intact. In fact, trail systems should be expanded whenever possible—we all own our public lands, and we all have a vested interest in the use of private land, especially private land with a history of community use. If we don't demand sufficient open space that provides enough trails, we'll end up like too many rats in a cage. That would be bad. If you have a problem with the way the land you cherish is being used or abused, write or call your elected representative or the land manager for the area in question (see page 39).

BEST FRIEND: DUCT TAPE

It's 6 p.m., and you're ten miles out in the backcountry. You have paid your climbing dues for five hours, and now it's time for the downhill plunge (controlled, of course); you figure you can still make it home for your hot date at 8 p.m. Unfortunately, when you shift down to climb a short hill, your derailleur shifts past the biggest cog—cunkkk—into the spokes of your rear wheel. The bike stops instantly, catapulting you toward that shrubbery on the side of the trail. Whoa, whoa, whoa. No physical damage, but your derailleur is cooked, and several of the spokes on your rear wheel look like spaghetti. Major malfunction. If you don't have a tool kit, you might spend the night in the woods and, worse yet, miss that dinner reservation. But if you have the right tools and know how to use them, you can probably still make it home.

Equipment damage can mean a long walk with a bike on your shoulder. Always carry a tool kit so you can fix anything from nine flats to a broken chain. Sometimes you'll need some imagination to concoct short-term fixes. A friend once filled his tire with pine cones to finish the ride because he didn't have any spare inner tubes. When I rode around the United States a number of years ago, I found that almost anything could be doctored, one way or another, if I had the four essentials—duct tape, vice grips, Super Glue, bailing wire (these items also kept my '69 Dodge Coronet wagon running for years).

Of course, some problems are even too big for these four essentials. You may find yourself ten miles out with a broken frame, a pretzeled wheel, or some other catastrophic failure. And there's not a water pack big enough to carry all the duct tape you'll need to fix a problem like that—thus the advice to carry water, food, flashlight, lighter, and extra clothes. Below is a suggested list of tools. Remember: Everyone's bike is different, so customize this list accordingly.

Recommended Tools

- pump
- patch kit
- extra tube
- tire irons
- spoke wrench
- chain tool
- Allen wrenches
- needle-nose pliers
- crescent wrench
- screwdriver
- spare brake cable

A quick repair on a dusty descent

LOST WITH ELVIS

Every year the summer tabloids feature a new round of incredible stories: Hikers getting eaten by bionic bats, miners spotting Elvis on a mule in the outback, and Bigfoot making a cameo at a Girl Scout sing-along. Fact or fiction on the newsstand, it's a sad truth of the trail: Many people end up lost, turned around, or off-course, headed in exactly the wrong direction just as the sun begins to set.

Supernatural phenomena aside, getting lost in the woods while riding a bike is easier than you might think. It's pretty easy to ride right by an unnoticed cairn or turn in the trail because you were, well, enjoying yourself. Just be sure to pay attention to your surroundings; watch the lay of the land. Frequently review your map while on unfamiliar trails. Whatever trail you're on, it's not Magic Mountain, so steel rails won't be returning you safely to the beginning of the ride.

Making notes on a new trail, circa 1898

Avoid Getting Lost

One: Gain an adequate knowledge of the area before leaving home. **Two:** Bring a map and compass and the skills to use them. **Three:** Watch the trail while riding (that's why you're out there!). **Four:** Stay home during severe weather. **Five:** Use good sense and stay on the main trail because the wrong trails—in the form of faint tracks, animal paths, long-abandoned railroad grades, and logging roads—are everywhere. In some areas, especially near mines, timber harvests, or off-road vehicle areas, jeep trails are as common as pine needles. Your brain must sift through the information—maps and trail descriptions, the sun, your compass, the lay of the land—and you must decide *not to get lost,* because, in the end, common sense is the best "gadget" you can bring.

If you do find yourself lost, don't panic. If you panic, you might as well subtract a few thousand dollars from your checkbook ledger for all the helicopter fuel it will take to find you. If lost, put on all your warm clothes, relax, and think with your cortex rather than your thalamus.

NIGHT RIDING

Although bicycle commuters have used sophisticated lighting systems for years, mountain biking at night was originally just the stealth way to poach closed trails. Then everyone realized that it was really, really fun, and night riding became more popular on all trails, legal and otherwise. Mountain bicyclists are now into urban night riding, full moon riding, and snow riding in the dark. But don't let the fun get in the way of being prepared—it's easier to get hurt or lost or cold in the middle of the night. (You don't want to know what it's like to repair a broken chain in the dark when the temperature is 10 degrees.)

The only holdup of a good lighting system is that it costs a lot of money. Many cyclists use two-beam, 16- to 20-watt systems, with a helmet-mounted light in addition to the standard, handlebar-mounted light. This is a nice way to go if your bank account can take the heat. If not, don't worry: You really only need about 10 watts to enjoy the experience.

Be forewarned, however, that night riding is technically illegal on most trails, even in areas open to mountain bikes. Many park systems and land management agencies prohibit nighttime use of their facilities, including trails. These laws were passed as tools to crack down on suspicious activity like drug dealing, and are rarely enforced on such benign users as mountain bicyclists (the Burke-Gilman Trail is technically closed at night). Still, it's best to know that if you go riding in the dark, it's probably against the law.

Night riding near Grand Ridge

RIDING TECHNIQUES

Many of the rides in *Kissing the Trail* don't require extreme riding skill or Herculean fitness, but some do. The technical advice that follows is for the rider who wants to smoothly transition from road riding to trail riding. Reality dictates that riding skills develop by trial and error (sorry). These suggestions ought to shrink the learning curve and minimize the number of times you eat dirt.

CADENCE: As a rule, try to pedal 70 to 100 rotations per minute while riding a bike. This can seem awkwardly fast if you're not used to "spinning" so quickly. But a healthy cadence is the easiest way to keep your legs fresh for the longest time possible. Slow, laborious pedal strokes strain muscles, tiring them out for the miles ahead. On tricky, irregular mountain terrain, the cadence rule doesn't always apply, but it's good to keep in mind. Using clipless pedals helps keep up an even, circular cadence (plus they keep your feet on the pedals). A good cadence is easiest to maintain when your seat has been adjusted properly—your knee should be slightly bent (like your mind) at the bottom of every pedal stroke.

Finishing a log crossing

DOWNHILL: The idea on any downhill pitch is not to flip forward over the front wheel. To accomplish this, adjust your seat down an inch or two and sit back to lower your center of gravity. In extreme cases, move your butt so it is actually behind the seat. Keep your arms and legs slightly bent, not locked, so they can function like shock absorbers. Keep your hands firmly and consistently on the brakes; you'll get nowhere waving one arm around like a cowboy. Don't use your front brake suddenly. Here's the Catch-22 of braking: The front brake does most of the real braking, *but* you have more precise steering *and* you're less likely to take a header if there is less pressure (or none) applied to the front wheel. Remember that speed is the most hazardous bicycling condition—it's difficult to get hurt at one mile per hour; at twenty miles per hour, it's all too easy.

UPHILL: The idea here is to get to the top the easiest way possible. During the transition between riding downhill or on a level and riding uphill, shift to a lower gear *before* you lose momentum. By maintaining a quick, even cadence throughout the transition, the hill will seem smoother and your legs won't lock as readily. During a steep climb, stay seated so your weight stays over the rear wheel—to keep it from spinning out. At the same time, make sure enough of your weight remains forward so that the front wheel doesn't pop up unexpectedly. On longer, more gradual hills, stand up occasionally—for power and also to give your muscles some variation—but be careful not to lose traction on the rear wheel. Finally, concentrate on deep, relaxed breathing; avoid locomotive breathing.

WATER: Inevitably, the mountain biker will come wheel to wheel with a body of water that needs to be navigated. And sometimes "navigate" is the right word when water reaches the seatpost and you're still thrashing and churning to stay vertical, hoping the current doesn't sweep you and the bike away. Here's what to do when you encounter a stream: **1.** Know what the bottom of the stream looks like; aim for the smoothest route across. **2.** Keep pedaling until you reach the opposite side. **3.** Pay attention to the environment; don't rage across delicate, dirt-bedded creeks— stop and carry your bike. This is critical during the fall when salmon are spawning, since even very shallow creeks can be salmon habitat. For puddles, though, it's best to ride straight through to prevent braiding (widening of the trail).

TECHNICAL RIDING: Rocks, roots, tight corners, switchbacks, billiard balls of horse pucky, drop-offs, encroaching foliage, gravel, logs, other trail users, sala-manders, all shapes and sizes of puddles—needless to say, there are times and places when the riding becomes technical and riding skills help tremendously. Although the proper ratio of balance and riding experience usually determines whether you'll get through a difficult section, these tips may help: **1.** Try standing up on the pedals at times. **2.** When it's rough, keep an iron grip on the handlebars. **3.** Grip the seat with your thighs on downhills. **4.** Always use your arms and legs as shock absorbers, not rebar. **5.** Keep pedaling!

WALKING YOUR BIKE: Walk the bike? This sounds like a non sequitur; the whole point of "bicycle" is that walking becomes extinct. Not. If you ride a mountain bike in the woods, you're bound to do some walking. Absolutely every serious mountain biker walks at some time, usually after trying to ride over a bus-sized rock or around a pit of poisonous snakes. Walking up a hill will almost always help extend the energy and spring in your already knotted legs, and it will make the remainder of the ride more enjoyable. Also, be cool to the earth: Walk to avoid damaging the trail.

BUYING A BICYCLE

The first decision you will need to make concerns the size of the check you want to write. Mountain bikes range in price from just under $200 to well over $5,000. How much to spend depends on your checkbook balance *and* the type of riding that you plan to do. Since this is a mountain bike guidebook, I assume you'll be out on dirt trails. For a basic mountain bike that performs with some degree of precision, you'll need to wring at least $450 from your account. At this price you can expect a lightweight frame, alloy wheels, an adequate set of components, and a responsible bike shop to help answer questions. In addition to the bike and sales tax, other goodies like a lock, a helmet, a pump, and this book can easily add $150 to the cost.

As the price of a bike goes up, two things happen—first, the weight of the bike drops and, second, the components last longer, perform better, and look cooler. Beyond the $2,000 threshold, you are paying for art. Up until that point, though, mountain bikes really do get lighter and better. Counterpoint: A $400 bike will get you there. In fact, I researched two mountain bike guides on $350 bicycles.

COMPONENTS: Components consist of everything but the frame and the wheels. A bike that costs more will come fitted with better components. Ask the salesperson to describe the differences between components on separate bikes. Then go to another store and ask another clerk to do the same. Look closely at the components—do they appear sturdy or cheap? If you are unsure why a part is attached to the bicycle you want to buy, have the salesperson explain its function. Give the brakes and derailleurs, the two component systems you'll be dealing with most, a good workout on the test ride.

The test ride

THE FRAME AND WHEELS: A lightweight frame and set of alloy wheels combine to make a more responsive, less fatiguing ride. Lighter bicycles make a dramatic difference when you are maneuvering tight corners, climbing hills, and accelerating. The feel of the bike depends on the frame materials and the architecture of the frame (tube lengths and angles). Although all frames look similar, an inch here or there can change the feel of the ride, especially if you have a particularly long pair of legs or short torso. Some frames provide a soft, comfortable ride; others offer a stiff, manic experience. Which feels best to you? Test ride, test ride, test ride.

SIZING A BIKE: When straddling a mountain bike, you should be able to lift it up about three or four inches. Choose a slightly larger bike if you plan to do most of your riding on the road, a smaller one if you want to concentrate on off-road riding. In addition to being lighter and stronger, smaller frames flex less than larger frames. Sometimes, though, a bigger frame just feels more comfortable. Be sure the salesperson fits you to each bike and adjusts the seat properly before the test ride. The real test is, of course, the test ride.

SUSPENSION: To suspend or not to suspend, that is the question. Most riders prefer front suspension to the feel of a rigid front fork. If you plan to ride primarily on trails, give your wrists, arms, and shoulders a break, and get a good front shock. Avoid the cheap shocks that may allow too much lateral flex and, thus, poor bike handling. Rear suspension comes in more flavors than Cliff Bars, and there's no consensus about which is best. Indeed, opinions vary about the benefits of having rear suspension at all, and it may depend as much on your riding style as anything else (oh yeah, and also your checkbook). If it feels right on the test ride, go for it.

THE TEST RIDE: Once you have decided on a price and size, and you have selected several bicycles that seem right, just whip out your checkbook and buy the one that looks the coolest. Hello? Put that checkbook away. It's time for the test ride. Take this part seriously; don't stop by the shop after work in a suit. Wear cycling clothes, and take your time.

When you ride the bike out of the store, don't just ride it around the block; try to ride the bike as though you already own it. Ride up and down steep hills, and pay attention to how the bike responds. Ask yourself some questions during the short time you have with the bike. Does your torso feel too scrunched or too stretched? How does the bike turn and shift and brake and accelerate? Some bikes will feel slow but stable, others will feel nimble but skittish. It's difficult to extrapolate from a short test ride to an eight-hour journey, but intuition is a pretty good judge. Buy what feels best.

AVOIDING THE BONK

Everyone wants to be able to hop on a bicycle and ride for miles without fatigue. And it seems possible to do, since the bicycle is the most efficient means of locomotion ever invented. Unfortunately for all of us, it doesn't exactly work that way. A long ride can make you tired. Much worse, though, is when a rider depletes all energy reserves before reaching the end of the trail and can't continue without a supreme effort: This is the dreaded bonk. It is possible, however, to get in shape so you can go dancing after a day's ride rather than go groping for the nearest couch.

There are three keys to mountain biking with less fatigue:

First, skilled riders expend less energy worrying, maneuvering, gripping the handle bars, starting, stopping. Practice riding skills such as balancing, riding over small objects, and tight turning. Good skills dramatically lessen ride fatigue.

Second, being in shape is also key. But being in shape doesn't mean riding a zillion miles at top speed; it means grooming your strength and endurance—and you need both out on the trail. If you lack one or the other, you'll bonk and your friends will abandon you because of your grumpiness. To improve endurance, ride on the flats for many hours with your pulse at or above 130 beats per minute. You should keep a quick cadence on these rides—you ought to be able to hold a conversation most of the way. To gain strength, go on rides that emphasize sprints, hills, and larger gears. These rides should be varied; at times your pulse should reach 90 percent of your maximum (220 minus your age). Try to put in at least a month of quality endurance riding before you begin the strength rides. To stay in reasonable mountain-biking shape, you need to exercise at least four times each week, two of which must be bicycling.

Third, eat properly while out on the trail. During the ride, take in plenty of fluids and calories. Eat and drink as much as you can. Carry a variety of food, and always carry more than you think you need. A candy bar or gel pack is handy for those times when you must have a whole bunch of calories in a hurry.

Now that you are in shape and eating the right things out on the trail, I'll wreck it by suggesting doughnuts and ropes of licorice. Junk food is the pirate of the food world, plundering our bodies with blank calories, heaps of sodium, and buckets of fat. But athletes like to argue that exercise mediates the downside of these rogue foods. Olympic marathon runner Don Kardong has said that without ice cream there would be darkness and chaos in the world. My question is: What about hamburgers, chips, red wine, and bulk cookies? Indeed, no rules regarding vices and mountain biking exist, though many a dogmatic personal trainer will lecture you differently. Aristotle urged us to search for a golden mean, a point between excesses, an elusive spot lying somewhere between many cookies and none.

MUD MAINTENANCE

How to keep the steed running smoothly? Although bikes run less well over time due to decrepit chains, worn cog teeth, old brakes and derailleurs, wobbly wheels, and stretched cables, we have a big maintenance challenge here in the Northwest: mud. Mud causes brakes to fail, derailleurs to stop functioning, bearings to grind to cubes, rims to peel, and, to add insult to injury, it weighs down the bike.

So what do you do about mud? Some shops tell you to let the mud dry, then wipe it off, so you won't taint your bike with water. Much too complicated and time consuming, especially in these climes. Besides, since my bike gets drenched during rides and soaked while on top of my car, how can a little hose-action hurt? Go ahead and hose the thing down, then dry it off with a rag. When the bearings grind square, replace them. Mud and clothes? Questions about laundry prove I have digressed a long way; however, since I'm here, let me note that there is not enough bleach on the planet to keep your riding socks white: Just concede the battle and wear black ones.

For other maintenance, the bike will usually let you know when things aren't running smoothly. Headsets, bottom brackets, cables, brake pads, tires, chains, square bearings, wheels, and freewheels are components to watch. When something doesn't feel as though it's working right, it's probably not. Every bike can and should run smoothly. Either fix it yourself or take it to a mechanic. But remember, it's a lot less painful to extract a $20 from your wallet now than to stand on the trail in a downpour, staring at a bike you *knew* needed repair.

Maintenance Suggestions
- Always keep your chain clean and lubricated.
- Always keep the brake pad surface flat (file them down) and brakes adjusted.
- Always keep the wheels true.
- Replace your chain every 800 miles.
- Replace your freewheel when the teeth look asymmetric.
- Replace tires, cables, and wheels when they look and/or feel worn.
- Repack bearings in hubs, bottom bracket, and headset twice a year. Okay, once.

ADVOCACY WORLD

Legislation is passed or discarded largely due to the number of calls and letters lawmakers receive on a given issue. Even nonelected officials make major decisions based on public input. Be a squeaky wheel and speak out for mountain bikers.

Clubs

Backcountry Bicycle Trails Club (BBTC)	www.bbtc.org
Cascade Bicycle Club	206-522-2407
International Mountain Bike Assoc. (IMBA)	303-545-9011
Single Track Mind	253-565-5124

Land Managers

King County Parks	206-296-4232
Mount Baker-Snoqualmie National Forest	
Snoqualmie Ranger District (Enumclaw)	360-825-6585
Snoqualmie Ranger District (North Bend)	425-888-1421
Mount Rainier National Park	360-569-2211
Washington State Department of Natural Resources	
Northwest Region	360-856-3500
South Puget Sound Region	360-825-1631
Washington State Parks	360-902-8844
Wenatchee National Forest	
Cle Elum Ranger District	509-674-4411
Snohomish County Parks	425-388-6600

USER FEE PRIMER

National Forests: You'll need a Northwest Forest Pass to park at most National Forest trailheads. You can buy a day pass or a yearly pass from outdoor retailers in the city and ranger stations and country groceries closer to the trailheads. You're likely to get a ticket if you park at a National Forest trailhead without one.

Mount Rainier National Park: Mount Rainier charges a vehicle fee when the ranger's on duty. You can also buy a year-long pass good for all national parks.

Washington State Parks: A Natural Investment Vehicle Parking Permit is required at most state park trailheads. Daily and yearly varieties are available. Most parks have a metal pay box, so you don't need to buy the permit in advance.

WEATHER

National Weather Service   www.wrh.noaa.gov/seattle

Destination 1 ✿✿✿✿✿

THE LAST DIRT TRAIL: RIP

Distance	**39.5 miles**, one-way shuttle
Terrain	Trails and roads, both dirt and paved; rolling hills, some walking
Duration	6 to 9 hours
Travel	18 miles from Seattle
Skill Level	Advanced
Season	Year round
Maps	USGS: *Bellevue North, Bellevue South, Carnation, Fall City*
Explorability	High
Restrictions	Some private property issues
More Info	Call Adventure Press for directions, 206-200-2578

Prelude

Check it out. Ten years ago you could ride from Woodinville to Issaquah almost entirely on dirt. It was called The Last Dirt Trail, and it was cool. Along its route you passed a lot of great, close-to-town mountain biking—the Redmond Watershed, Beaver Lake, the Northwest Passage, Grand Ridge, and more. Development

and closures morphed that trail into the Son of the Last Dirt Trail for the second edition of *Kissing the Trail*. In that incarnation, the journey went via Tolt-MacDonald Park and the Snoqualmie Valley Trail but included a fair amount of pavement. Today you can still go to some of these places (kind of) and you can still explore your way from Woodinville to Issaquah on dirt (less) and pavement (more), but by and large the trail is dead, paved over and topped off with large suburban houses, blocked by fences and No Trespassing signs. Of course during the same time, superfun user-built trails have taken over from nutty suburban exploring anyway. And the evolution of mountain biking continues...

Goodbye to The Last Dirt Trail

Ride 2 ⊛ ⊛ ⊛

GRAND RIDGE

Distance	**6.0 miles**, out and back
Terrain	Dirt trails, gravel rail-trail; some steep hills, **cumulative gain: 900 ft.**
Duration	1 to 2 hours
Travel	20 miles from Seattle
Skill Level	Intermediate
Season	Year round
Maps	USGS: *Fall City, Bellevue South*
Explorability	Moderate
Restrictions	Watch out for private property, day-use only
More Info	King County Parks, 206-296-4232, www.metrokc.gov/parks/

Prelude

Hey, remember Grand Ridge? Two minutes from Issaquah? It used to be one of the hot mountain bike areas close to town. Nowadays, you hardly ever even see a car in the small parking area. But there's a fun new trail up there, through alder and Douglas fir forest, and the area's proximity makes it perfect for a short, post-work ride. After a nice warm-up along a rail-trail, the singletrack climb on this 6-mile out and back can take your wind away. The tread ranges from compact to muddy. A gigantic housing development has come to a large part of Grand Ridge, obliterating a number of the classic trails. But King County Parks has said that new trails and mountain bikes are part of the plan up there. Stay tuned. In the meantime, there's no reason to stay away, although there have been reports of car prowls at the trailhead—see the directions below for alternative parking.

Following the trail at Grand Ridge

Driving Directions

Drive east on Interstate 90 past Issaquah to Exit 20, the High Point Exit. At the end of the ramp, turn left, go under the freeway, past the entrance ramp, then park immediately in the small dirt area on the left. Alternative: Turn right at the end of the ramp then immediately right again. This is the entrance road to Tiger Mountain. Park with the hikers alongside this road and ride the one quarter-mile back to the Grand Ridge Trailhead.

The Ride

From the parking area, ride across the gated bridge above the East Fork of Issaquah Creek. Pedal down the wide railroad grade, descending slightly. At **1.1 miles**, find two trails on the right that cut up the hill away from the railroad grade. Take the right-hand trail.

After about 50 yards, the two trails meet and become one again. Almost immediately the trail forks—take the right fork. The climb begins here, and small

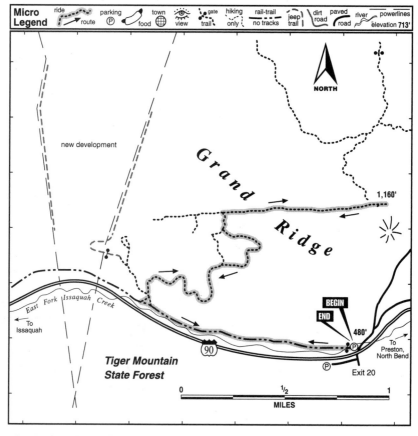

Railroad grade access to Grand Ridge

gears and a high pain threshold are suddenly a good thing. During the climb you'll have to dismount to cross a creek. Then at **1.6 miles**, reach a fork and bear right. The grade is somewhat easier here as the trail winds upward through the trees. When you reach a T at **2.1 miles**, turn right. The trail bounces across a small Grand Ridge shoulder then hits another T at **2.4 miles**—turn right onto the wider trail and begin a steep climb.

This wide trail, the remnants of an old road, ascends at a brutal rate then levels then ascends again. The sometimes muddy, sometimes rocky tread makes this section more difficult. Cross dirt roads at **2.6 miles** and **2.9 miles**. Ignore a trail on the left. At **3.0 miles**, reach the top of Grand Ridge. From here, just turn around and ride back, unless you feel like exploring.

NOTES:

_____

_____

_____

_____

Ride 3 ⨀⨁⨀

ISSAQUAH TO GRAND RIDGE

Distance	**13.2 miles**, out and back
Terrain	Dirt roads, singletrack; two hard climbs, **cumulative gain: 1,500 ft.**
Duration	2 to 3 hours
Travel	19 miles from Seattle
Skill Level	Intermediate
Season	Year round
Map	Department of Natural Resources: *Tiger Mountain State Forest*
Explorability	Moderate
Restrictions	Watch out for private property and hiker-only trails
More Info	King County Parks, 206-296-4232, www.metrokc.gov/parks/

Prelude

This ride has changed from previous editions of *Kissing the Trail*. For that, you can blame/thank the Sunset Interchange. Rather than being a loop beginning and ending in Issaquah, it's now an out and back to the top of Grand Ridge. In truth, it's probably a better ride now. An intermediate ride over varied terrain, from urban edge to forested ridgetop, this ride is perfect for a strong, beginning rider or a more advanced rider with limited time. Since it begins in downtown Issaquah, some cyclists can ride to the trailhead, and that's a good thing. A little history on the Old Bus Road Trail featured here: After using grant money to reconstruct the trail to multi-use (including bicycle) standards, the DNR closed it to bikes. Flat, short, and with the ancient bus still rusting along the way, there's no reason bicycles should be banned from this old road.

Driving Directions

Take Interstate 90 east to Exit 17 in Issaquah. Zero out your odometer at the end of the exit ramp, and turn right onto Front Street. At 0.6 mile, turn left on Sunset Way. At 0.8 mile, turn right on 2nd Avenue S.E. At 1.0 mile, turn right on S.E. Clark Street. Immediately turn left and park in the lot at the community center.

The Ride

From the community center, head south, away from downtown Issaquah, on a paved rail-trail. At **0.2 mile**, the trail bends to the left and crosses 2nd Avenue S.E. Continue straight across the road to the trail, now dirt, on the opposite side. Just

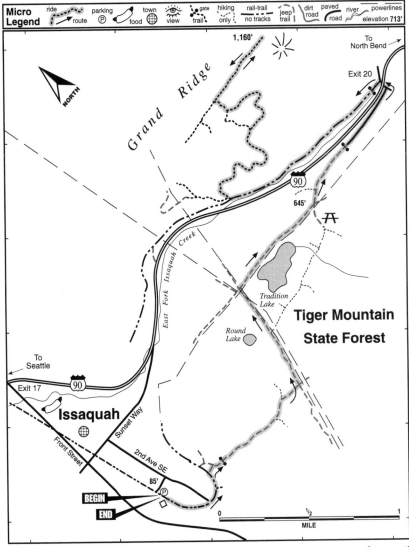

1,160'

Grand Ridge

To North Bend

Exit 20

90

645'

East Fork Issaquah Creek

Tradition Lake

Round Lake

Tiger Mountain

State Forest

To Seattle

Exit 17

90

Issaquah

Sunset Way

2nd Ave SE

Front Street

85'

℗

BEGIN

END

0   ½   1

MILE

beyond this crossing, the trail meets a set of power lines, **0.4 mile**. Ignore a faint trail or two, but then take the first real right onto an old jeep road. The road climbs to a metal gate at **0.5 mile**; a sign explains that bicycles are allowed on posted trails only. After a serious climb up a rocky, dirt road through a wooded area, ignore the trail off to the right, **1.1 miles**. Continue up the main road.

The jeep road narrows and several promising singletracks spur off, but continue up the main trail. Emerge from the forested area and bear up to the left, following a set of power lines. At **1.3 miles**, reach the top of the hill at a power-line tower.

Trail near the high school

At **1.6 miles**, ignore the Old Bus Road Trail on the right and continue straight, underneath the power lines. The jeep trail divides for a time—take either fork and continue under the power lines. Reach a 4-way intersection at **2.0 miles** and turn right, following yet another set of power lines. Pedal along the gravel road, passing Lake Tradition on the right.

At **2.7 miles**, reach another 4-way intersection and turn left. Ride down the gravel road to a gate and parking area, **3.1 miles**. Pass through the gate and proceed along the paved road. At 3.5 miles, turn left onto 270th S.E. and ride under Interstate 90. Immediately after passing the westbound entrance, turn left into a small dirt parking area, **3.6 miles** (see Ride 2).

Cross a short bridge at the back of the parking area, and head down the wide, gravel railroad grade, descending slightly. At **4.7 miles**, find two trails on the right that cut up the hill away from the railroad grade. Take the right-hand trail.

After about 50 yards, the two trails meet and become one again. Almost immediately the trail forks—take the right fork. The climb begins here, and small gears and a high pain threshold are suddenly a good thing. It's all ridable, except for about halfway up where you'll have to dismount to cross a creek. At **5.2 miles**, reach a fork and bear right. The grade is somewhat easier here as the trail winds upward through the trees. When you reach a T at **5.7 miles**, turn right. The trail bounces across a small Grand Ridge shoulder then hits another T at **6.0 miles**—turn right onto the wider trail and begin another steep climb.

This wide trail, the remnants of an old road, ascends at a brutal rate, levels off then ascends again. The sometimes muddy, sometimes rocky tread makes this section more of a challenge. Cross dirt roads at **6.2 miles** and **6.5 miles**. Ignore a trail on the left, then almost immediately, **6.6 miles**, reach the top of Grand Ridge. Now it's time to turn around and head back, unless you feel like exploring.

NOTES:

_____

_____

_____

_____

Ride 4 ✿ ✿ ✿ ✿

PRESTON RAILROAD GRADE

Distance	**11.6 miles**, lollipop loop
Terrain	Singletrack, dirt roads; steep climbs, **cumulative gain: 1,550 ft.**
Duration	2 to 4 hours
Travel	29 miles from Seattle
Skill Level	Advanced
Season	Late spring, summer, fall
Map	Green Trails: *Tiger Mountain 204S*
Explorability	Moderate
Restrictions	Closed October 15 to April 15
More Info	Washington State Department of Natural Resources, South Puget Sound Region, 360-825-1631, www.wa.gov/dnr/

Prelude

In the early 1990s, the Backcountry Bicycle Trails Club scouted and built this trail, and it is still maintained primarily by members of the BBTC. The trail offers an excellent Northwest mix of smooth zippies and snake-bite root gardens through thick forest. The end of the loop con-nects with the Northwest Timber Trail, one of the sweetest sections of trail anywhere. These trails are overcrowded, and it's a shame and a disgrace that the DNR hasn't opened more trails to bi-cycles on East and South Tiger Moun-tain. The first three miles climb steeply up a nondescript dirt road on East Tiger Mountain's south flank. On clear days, a few long views assist with the climb; on not so good days, you'll have to gut it out until you hit the trail. Next comes the Preston Railroad Grade, part swoopy singletrack, part logging rail-

road grade built early in the twentieth century, and now one of the best known and most jarring trails in King County. Check out Options below for a great three-mile addition to the ride.

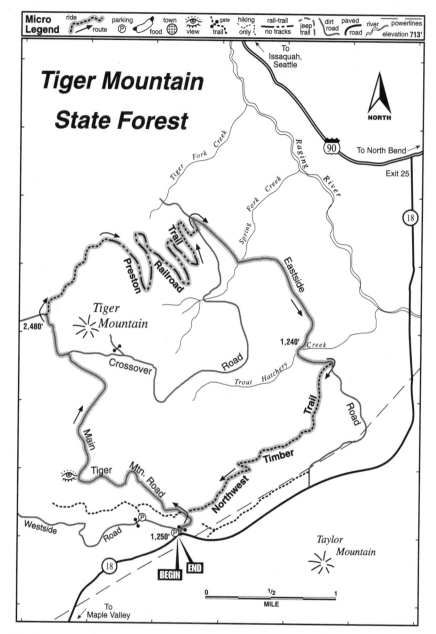

Driving Directions

From Seattle, drive east on Interstate 90 to Exit 25, the Highway 18 Exit. Hit your trip odometer at the end of the exit ramp and turn right, heading south on Highway 18. At 4.3 miles, immediately after Tiger Summit, turn in to the parking

The Preston begins

area on the right. Note: Most people park in the lot adjacent to Hwy 18. However, if you head up the left-hand road a quarter-mile, you'll find a second parking area—something to consider given the number of car break-ins I hear about at Tiger.

The Ride

Two dirt roads exit from the north end of the parking lot. Take the gated road on the right. Immediately the grade becomes steep, winding up the south side of East Tiger Mountain. Pass the Northwest Timber Trail on the right at **0.3 mile**. Pass the Connector Trail on the left, a few pedal strokes farther. Continue up the road, a steep climb. Reach a viewpoint (a rest point!) at **1.4 miles**. From here you get great views of Mount Rainier as well as the Green, Cedar, and White River valleys. Though the worst of the climbing is now over, the grade continues off and on, climbing to a T at **2.8 miles**. Take a left (the right fork leads to the top of East Tiger in 1.4 miles, where you'll find the pleasant combination of picnic tables and microwave towers).

Whoa—at **3.2 miles** find the Preston Railroad Trail on the right. This turn is easily missed by anyone who has drifted deep into hallucinations due to lack of oxygen from the long climb. The smooth trail swoops and whorls through the deep forest, dropping and climbing until it meets what remains of the old Preston railroad grade at **3.9 miles**. The railroad grade, straight and evenly sloped compared to the earlier trail, switchbacks down the west side of Tiger Mountain, descending rapidly along a bumpy and jarring tread. Blowdown, wet rocks, and one Barnum-and-Bailey root circus after another make long sections of this trail difficult, especially in wet weather. For lesser skilled riders, some walking is inevitable. For reference, the trail switchbacks at **4.6 miles**, **5.1 miles**, **5.6 miles**, **5.9 miles**, **6.3 miles**, and **6.5 miles** before S-curving out to a road.

Straightaway on the NW Timber Trail

At **6.9 miles**, reach the road, and take a left, downhill. (Want to ride the Preston again? Turn right and ride 3.4 miles up the Crossover Road, and you'll reach the T at 2.8 miles.) Ride a short distance to another road at **7.1 miles**. This time turn right and traverse gradually down. Ignore a lesser road back on the right at **7.9 miles**. At **8.8 miles**, after a steep final descent, the road bottoms out and heads up. At the top of the hill, **9.0 miles**, find the Northwest Timber Trail on the right. **Whoa**—it's easy to miss. The ride along the (mostly) easy grades of this wonderful (though overused) trail is fun, fun, fun. After numerous bridge crossings and a few hairy corners, reach the Main Tiger Mountain Road at **11.4 miles**. Turn left and ride down to the parking area, **11.6 miles**.

Options

One: Ride out the Northwest Timber Trail, along the Eastside Road, then up the Preston Railroad Trail. When you get to the top, turn around and ride back, 16.8 miles total. **Two**: Ride the Iverson Railroad Trail and then ride the Preston. Follow the Iverson directions to the T at 3.1 miles. Turn left and ride the excellent Connector Trail to Tiger Mountain Road, 3.4 miles. You're now 0.3 mile above the parking area and into the Preston ride. Turn left and climb up the road to the Preston Railroad Trail. If you started from the parking lot adjacent to Hwy 18, the total is 15.0 miles.

NOTES:

_____

_____

_____

_____

Ride 5 ✸ ✸ ✸

IVERSON RAILROAD GRADE

Distance	**3.2 miles,** loop (longer options)
Terrain	Singletrack, gravel roads; some steep climbs, **cumulative gain: 750 ft.**
Duration	1 hour
Travel	29 miles from Seattle
Skill Level	Advanced
Season	Late spring, summer, fall
Map	Green Trails: *Tiger Mountain 204S*
Explorability	Moderate
Restrictions	Closed October 15 to April 15
More Info	Washington State Department of Natural Resources, South Puget Sound Region, 360-825-1631, www.wa.gov/dnr/

Prelude

The Iverson Railroad Grade, a.k.a. the Fat Hand Trail, is short but loads of fun, with winding traverses, short hectic climbs, and technical descents. After a warm-up along Westside Road, the route accesses a trail which traverses through the forests of Tiger Mountain's south side. As with the Northwest Timber Trail and the Preston Railroad Trail, members of the Backcountry Bicycle Trails Club and others from the cycling community helped design and build the Iverson Railroad Trail.

Gliding along the Iverson Railroad Trail

Driving Directions

From Seattle, drive east on Interstate 90 to Exit 25, the Highway 18 Exit. Hit your trip odometer at the end of the exit ramp and turn right, heading south on Hwy 18. At 4.3 miles, immediately after Tiger Summit, turn in to the parking area on the right. From the north end of the lot, take the left-hand road. At 4.6 miles, reach the trailhead parking on the right.

It's all good on the Iverson

The Ride

The parking area serves as the trailhead for the Iverson Railroad Trail (Fat Hand Trail). Instead of taking the trail, begin this ride by pedaling up the Westside Road. Turn right on the road, then immediately pass around a gate. At **0.2 mile**, reach a fork and bear right. The road rolls up and down, and is steep in places. At **0.5 mile**, crest the hill and glide down to the upper trailhead of the Iverson Railroad Trail on the right, **1.3 miles**.

Take the smooth singletrack, which climbs for a moment, noodles, then climbs again. It's a beautiful, easily ridable trail. At **1.8 miles**, pass over a high point. From here, the trail continues traversing east. When the trail divides at **2.4 miles**, take the right fork and corkscrew downward. Ignore a lesser trail on the left at **2.5 miles**. From here the way is more technical, the rocks and roots bigger and the descent steep. The trail crosses a series of short bridges as you drop and climb in what seems a willy-nilly way.

Reach a T at **3.1 miles**—take the right fork (the left fork, the Connector Trail, connects the Iverson Railroad Trail to the Northwest Timber Trail after about one quarter-mile). The right fork drops to the parking area at **3.2 miles**.

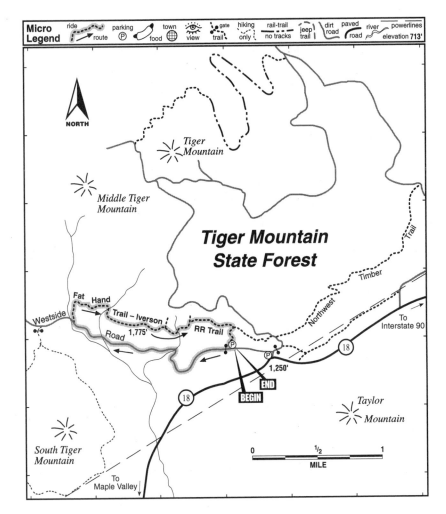

Options

You can can add five miles to this route by including an out-and-back on the Connector Trail and the Northwest Timber Trail (check out the map). But the best idea is to combine the Iverson with the Preston Railroad Trail for a 14.5-mile loop (see Ride 4). Ride the Iverson, then take the Connector Trail to Tiger Mountain Road and turn left. You are now about one quarter-mile into Ride 4.

NOTES:

Ride 6 ✇ ✇ ✇

CROSSOVER ROAD

Distance	**11 miles**, loop
Terrain	Dirt and gravel roads; long steep climbs, **cumulative gain: 1,550 ft.**
Duration	2 to 3 hours
Travel	29 miles from Seattle
Skill Level	Intermediate
Season	Year round
Map	Green Trails: *Tiger Mountain 204S*
Explorability	Moderate
Restrictions	None
More Info	Washington State Department of Natural Resources, South Puget Sound Region, 360-825-1631, www.wa.gov/dnr/

Prelude

For all the wrong reasons, Tiger Mountain singletrack is closed to bikes six months out of the year. With a cynical attempt at fairness, the closures affect all users on trails open to bicycles; however, none of Tiger's hiker-only trails are closed at any time. So from mid-October to mid-April, where can you ride? Well, from the same parking area on East Tiger that accesses the Preston Railroad Trail (see Ride 4) and the Iverson Railroad Trail (see Ride 5), you can ride several of the gated dirt roads on the mountain. This is essentially a road version of the Preston Railroad Trail loop, substituting Crossover Road for the trail and the power-line trail for the Northwest Timber Trail. No singletrack, but you can count on a good workout.

Driving Directions

From Seattle, drive east on Interstate 90 to Exit 25, the Highway 18 Exit. Zero your odometer at the end of the exit ramp and turn right, heading south on Hwy 18. At 4.3 miles, immediately after Tiger Summit, turn in to the parking area on the right. Note: Most people park in the lot adjacent to Hwy 18. If you head up the left-hand road one quarter-mile, however, you'll find a second parking area— something to consider given the number of car break-ins I hear about at Tiger.

The Ride

Two dirt roads exit from the northeast corner of the parking area. Take the road on the right, the Main Tiger Mountain Road, which is gated. Immediately the grade

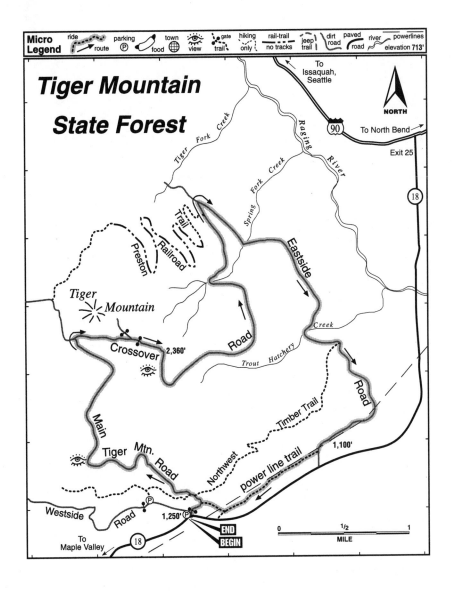

Tiger Mountain State Forest

Micro Legend: ride · route · parking ℗ · town · food · view · gate · hiking trail · hiking only · rail-trail no tracks · jeep trail · dirt road · paved road · river · powerlines · elevation 713'

To Issaquah, Seattle

NORTH

90

To North Bend

Exit 25

18

Tiger Fork Creek

Raging River

Spring Fork Creek

Trail

Railroad

Preston

Tiger Mountain

Crossover 2,360'

Eastside

Road

Creek

Trout Hatchery

Timber Trail

Main Tiger Mtn. Road

Northwest

power line trail

1,100'

Road

Westside Road

1,250' ℗

END
BEGIN

To Maple Valley

18

0   1/2   1
MILE

becomes steep, winding up the south side of East Tiger Mountain. In rapid succession, pass an unmarked trail on the right, **0.1 mile**, the Northwest Timber Trail on the right, **0.25 mile**, and the (weakly named) Connector Trail on the left, **0.3 mile**. Continue up the road, a steep climb with only a few short breaks in the grade. Reach an overlook at **1.5 miles**, affording great views of Mount Rainier as well as the Green, Cedar, and White River valleys. Though the worst of the climbing is over, the grade continues to climb to a T at **2.8 miles**.

Climbing Tiger Mountain

Take the road to the right, the Crossover Road, following the sign toward East Tiger Summit. Here the grade steepens and your little front chainring is again your friend. The road levels out at **3.3 miles**. Then, at **3.4 miles**, the road forks. (The left fork heads to the summit, located about 0.8 mile farther up.) Bear right, climb a short hill, and reach the ride's high point at **3.5 miles**. From the top, descend sharply to **4.8 miles** where the road levels to traverse east. After a steep drop around the **5.6-mile** mark, Crossover Road passes the Preston Railroad Trail on the left, **6.2 miles**. Reach a T in the road at **6.3 miles** and turn right onto the East Side Road.

The East Side Road traverses back toward the south side of the mountain. Stay on the main road. Soon afterwards, **7.8 miles**, the road drops precipitously for a short distance, crosses the lovely Trout Hatchery Creek, then begins a short climb. At the top of the hill, **8.3 miles**, pass the entrance to the Northwest Timber Trail on the right—continue straight. The road descends, then climbs, then descends again to a large set of power lines at **9.0 miles**. Continue down the road, which passes under the power lines then bears to the right, paralleling them.

Whoa—when the road forks at **9.6 miles**, turn right onto the lesser road, and climb steeply underneath the power lines. (If you reach Highway 18, you have gone one quarter-mile too far.) At **9.9 miles**, the jeep trail appears to fork at the base of one of the power line towers. Take the left fork, cutting around and below the tower on the left. The rough trail continues under the power lines, dropping then climbing again. Most riders will have to walk part of the next climb.

Pass a faint trail on the right; then at **10.7 miles**, take a singletrack to the right that crosses under the power lines and enters a dark section of woods (again, if you reach Highway 18, you have gone too far). Ride through the woods for less than one quarter-mile, then pop out onto the Main Tiger Mountain Road. Turn left, returning to the parking lot at **11.0 miles**.

NOTES:

_____

_____

Ride 7 🌼🌼🌼🌼

POO POO POINT

Distance	**14 miles**, out and back
Terrain	Gravel and dirt road; long steep climbs, **cumulative gain: 2,600 ft.**
Duration	2 to 4 hours
Travel	29 miles from Seattle
Skill Level	Intermediate
Season	Year round
Map	Green Trails: *Tiger Mountain 204S*
Explorability	Low
Restrictions	None
More Info	Washington State Department of Natural Resources, South Puget Sound Region, 360-825-1631, www.wa.gov/dnr/

Prelude

Steeper grades and a heftier elevation gain make the ride up Tiger Mountain's West Side Road—to Poo Poo Point—more difficult than Crossover Road (see Ride 6). The last two-mile pitch to the top will wreak havoc with your quads, but the views from Poo Poo Point—jumping point for hang gliders and parasailers—are epic. Odds are, though, that you've selected this dirt road ride because the trails on Tiger Mountain are closed between October and April, so what is the chance that you'll have clear weather to enjoy the view? Keep telling yourself it's a training ride. From the end of the West Side Road at Poo Poo Point, a hiker/equestrian trail connects with the High School Trail near Issaquah (see Ride 3). If this trail were open to mountain bikes, you could ride almost completely around Tiger Mountain on dirt, a "Wonderland Trail" of sorts. Wouldn't that be cool?

Driving Directions

From Seattle, drive east on Interstate 90 to Exit 25, the Highway 18 Exit. Hit your trip odometer at the end of the exit ramp and turn right, heading south on Hwy 18. At 4.3 miles, immediately after Tiger Summit, turn in to the parking area on the right. From the north end of the lot, take the left-hand road. At 4.6 miles, reach the trailhead parking on the right.

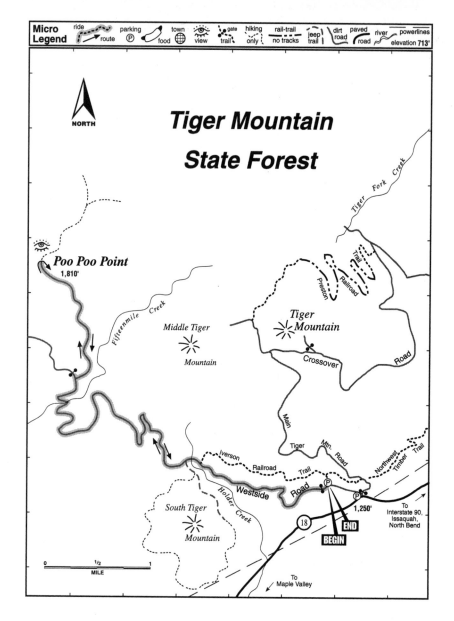

Micro Legend

ride route · parking (P) · town food ⊕ · view · gate · hiking trail only · rail-trail no tracks · jeep trail · dirt road · paved road · river · powerlines · elevation 713'

Tiger Mountain

State Forest

NORTH

Tiger Fork Creek

Poo Poo Point
1,810'

Fifteenmile Creek

Middle Tiger
Mountain

Preston · Railroad · Trail

Tiger Mountain

Crossover

Road

Main

Iverson Railroad Trail

Tiger Mtn. Road

Northwest Timber Trail

Westside Road

Holder Creek

South Tiger Mountain

18

1,250'

END

BEGIN

To Interstate 90, Issaquah, North Bend

0   1/2   1
MILE

To Maple Valley

The Ride

From the parking area, turn right, ride around a gate, and pedal up the West Side Road. At **0.2 miles**, the road forks—bear right. From here, the road rolls, gets steep, then rolls some more. Cross over a high point at **0.5 mile**. Descend for a time, passing the upper entrance to the Iverson Railroad Trail (see Ride 5) on the right

Onward toward Poo Poo Point

at **1.3 miles**. The road turns upward again, following Holder Creek for a short distance. At the **1.5-mile** mark, pass the South Tiger Loop Trail on the left. This is a hiker/equestrian trail, but it ought to be open to mountain bikes to help disperse the overuse of the Preston Railroad Trail and the Northwest Timber Trail.

Continue climbing and at **2.0 miles** reach a second high point. From here, the road drops quickly through lush forest, affording some territorial views. A couple of trails and at least one road exit the Westside Road during this stretch, so stay on the main road. **Whoa**—watch for a dangerous gate that is located around a blind downhill corner, **4.7 miles**. Just past the gate, drop to the bridge across Fifteenmile Creek.

From Fifteenmile Creek, the really strenuous climb to Poo Poo Point begins. Take the right fork at **5.0 miles** and continue climbing. Over the next two miles, the road ascends 500 feet per mile—ouch. Just after the road levels, take the right fork at **6.8 miles**, then spin easily over the final stretch to the vista at Poo Poo Point, **7.0 miles**. After enjoying the view, retrace your pedal strokes back to the parking area near Tiger Mountain Summit, **14.0 miles**.

NOTES:

_____

_____

_____

_____

Ride 8 ✦✦✦

CCC ROAD

Distance	**20 miles**, out and back (longer and shorter options)
Terrain	Dirt roads, doubletrack, some trail; **cumulative gain: 1,600 ft.**
Duration	4 to 6 hours
Travel	37 miles from Seattle
Skill Level	Intermediate
Season	Spring, summer, fall
Maps	Green Trails: *Bandera, Mount Si*
Explorability	Moderate
Restrictions	None
More Info	Mount Baker-Snoqualmie National Forest, Snoqualmie District (North Bend), 425-888-1421, www.fs.fed.us/r6/mbs/

Prelude

Every time I go ride the CCC Road I'm always taken by surprise at how much fun it is because it's just that: a road. But it's gated at both ends, and though motorized vehicles use some parts of it (legally and otherwise), you'll find few motors on this ride. Several sections are simply not used by anyone, due to washouts and lack of use, and alders are doing their best to eliminate the road in a flurry of growth. Over the first few miles, you'll find a wide gravel road that ascends a stiff hill and then meanders through old clearcuts, which afford occasional views of Garfield Mountain across the valley; later you'll bounce down rocky doubletrack and carry your bike around blowdown. As of the beginning of 2003, the last few miles are almost unridable due to the overgrowth—saplings slap at your face, blackberry vines buzzsaw at your arms and legs. The Forest Service plans to upgrade this section, but the timetable for this work keeps changing. In the meantime, you might consider turning around at the 7.2-mile point or be prepared for a wild, sometimes frustrating adventure. And no one would mind if you brought along a machete and did a little trimming while you were out there. So while certainly not all singletrack, the CCC Road is a worthwhile ride, and exactly the kind of tread that can handle year-round use.

Stuck in the trees. Doh!

Sunny morning on the CCC Road

Driving Directions

From Seattle, take Interstate 90 eastbound to Exit 31 at North Bend. At the end of the exit ramp, set your odometer to zero and turn left onto Bendigo Boulevard S. At 0.7 miles, turn right onto North Bend Way. At 2.0 miles, take a left onto S.E. Mount Si Road. Stay on the main road as it twists and bends. Pass the Mount Si Trailhead at 4.7 miles. At 5.9 miles, find an unmarked, gated road on the left and park. If this small area is full, retreat to the Mount Si Trailhead parking area.

The Ride

Whoa—do not ride up the gated road (to Mount Teneriffe). Instead, continue out the paved road on your bike. Just after the gravel pulloff, the hill begins. After **0.25 mile**, the road becomes gravel, and continues its steep upward cant. After gaining more than 300 feet of elevation, the road levels somewhat, **0.75 mile**. Ignore several lesser spurs off the main road, then at **1.1 miles** reach a gate across the road. Pass around the gate and continue up, sticking to the main road.

Woof! Reach a 4-way intersection at the top of the hill (and the top of the ride), **2.1 miles**. From the crest of the hill you can see Mount Garfield and views of the Middle Fork of the Snoqualmie River valley through the trees. Travel straight through the intersection on the main road. The road, now a doubletrack, rounds the southern edge of a small plateau as it gradually descends. At **3.0 miles**, the doubletrack forks—go left. Continue on the obvious main route, then bear right at a fork at **3.7 miles**. The plateau gives way to a steep hillside just before a stream crossing, and the doubletrack, now more primitive, traverses the steep slope and enters a darker forest, **4.4 miles**. The way is rocky in places.

From here, the gradual downhill traverse follows a mostly smooth jeep trail through a nice forest. The trail crosses several small creeks, some diverted through culverts, which carry water to the Middle Fork of the Snoqualmie. At **6.8 miles**, cross a substantial creek. Just past the crossing, the road forks. Both forks are wider and less primitive than the last few miles of trail have been. (The right fork drops down to the Middle Fork Road in slightly more than one mile.) Take the left fork (straight).

As the road bends to the left, **7.2 miles**, reach another fork. **Whoa**—take the easy-to-miss right fork, an old grassy jeep trail. Here's where this ride really gets

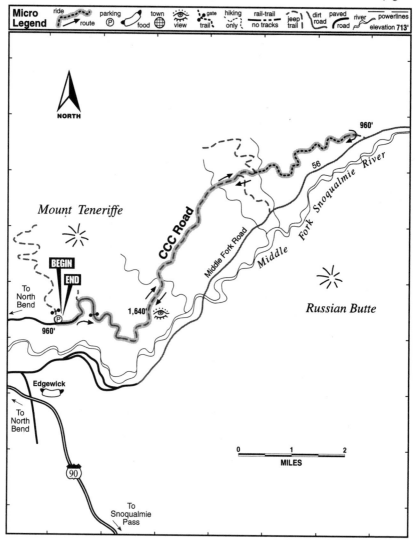

interesting. Since the jeep trail hasn't been used much, young alder and Douglas Fir saplings have grown up from the trail's tread; shrubs and vines have filled in the corridor from the sides. Though kind of ridable (with eye protection), this section is in serious need of brushing the growth away from the trail. In spots the tread seems to vanish.

Continue pedaling downward on the rough trail. At **9.5 miles** reach a huge rockfall that has obliterated the trail. Walk over the boulders to the trail on the opposite side. At **9.6 miles**, reach a T and turn downhill to the right. After a short but steep and rocky descent, arrive at the Middle Fork Road, **10.0 miles**. From the Middle Fork Road, turn around and retrace your tracks to the parking area at the gate to Mount Teneriffe, **20.0 miles**.

Options

One: A loop can be constructed by turning right on the Middle Fork Road and taking it back into North Bend (see the last 18 miles of Ride 14). **Two:** Another option, designed to bypass the most difficult section of the CCC Road, is to turn right and ride just over two miles down the Middle Fork Road, then turn right onto a dirt road. Pedal up this dirt road just over one mile and turn left onto the CCC Road—you're now back at the creek crossing noted at 6.8 miles. **Three:** Turn around at the 7.2-mile point to avoid the overgrown trail. For more options, see Rides 9 and 14).

NOTES:

_____

_____

_____

_____

CCC EXTENSION

Distance	**5.7 miles**, loop
Terrain	Dirt trails, dirt roads; short hills, **cumulative gain: 400 ft.**
Duration	1 to 2 hours
Travel	46 miles from Seattle
Skill Level	Intermediate
Season	Summer, early fall
Maps	Green Trails: *Bandera, Mount Si*
Explorability	Moderate
Restrictions	NW Forest Pass, possible seasonal closure
More Info	Mount Baker-Snoqualmie National Forest, Snoqualmie District (North Bend), 425-888-1421, www.fs.fed.us/r6/mbs/

Prelude

The Forest Service began construction on the CCC Extension Trail during the summer of 2002, but as of January 2003 it was neither open nor complete. It is ridable, however, and it should be open starting sometime during summer 2003. It's an easy trail—wide, short, with not much elevation gain—but it's a fun one. And despite all the delays and trail-user bickering, it's a new trail in the Middle Fork valley. Wow! Note: Since it hasn't officially opened, the restrictions weren't set when this book went to press. There may be a seasonal closure. Call ahead for details.

Driving Directions

From Seattle, take Interstate 90 eastbound to Exit 34. At the end of the exit ramp, set your odometer to zero and turn left on S.E. Edgewick Road. At 0.4 mile, turn right onto S.E. Middle Fork Road (becomes Forest Road 56). Reach a fork at 1.4 miles, and stay right. At 3 miles, the road becomes dirt, and it can be rough from here on out. At 12.4 miles, find the large dirt parking area for the Middle Fork trailhead on the right.

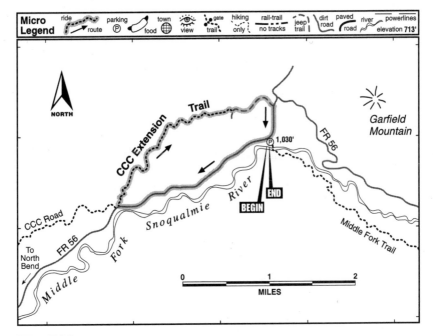

The Ride

From the Middle Fork Trail's parking area, ride out to the Middle Fork Road (FR 56) and turn left. Flat and wide, the road functions as a nice warm-up. At **2.2 miles**, find the beginning of the CCC Extension Trail back on the right. The trail immediately begins climbing the hillside away from the Middle Fork Road.

After several switchies and windies up the embankment, the trail bends to the right and levels. At **2.6 miles**, reach a 4-way intersection and go straight, now pedaling along a jeep trail. At **3.2 miles**, the CCC Extension Trail starts up again on the left. Take it. From here, the trail winds through a dark forest, crossing several short bridges along the way. It's a fun section of new trail.

The trail ends at a rocky jeep road at **4.7 miles**. (The Forest Service plans to continue the singletrack from here down to the Middle Fork Road near the trailhead, but the completion date is uncertain.) Bear left on the rocky jeep road and bounce down a gradual slope. Reach a gravel pit at **5.1 miles**. Continue down the primary road, which is now dirt, until you arrive at the Middle Fork Road, **5.3 miles**. Turn right and ride down to the Middle Fork trailhead, **5.7 miles**, to complete the loop.

NOTES:

Ride 10 ✿ ✿ ✿

MIDDLE FORK OF THE SNOQUALMIE RIVER

Distance	**13 miles**, loop
Terrain	Dirt trails, dirt roads; some steep climbs, **cumulative gain: 1,100 ft.**
Duration	2 to 4 hours
Travel	46 miles from Seattle
Skill Level	Intermediate
Season	Summer, early fall
Maps	Green Trails: *Skykomish, Mount Si*
Explorability	Low
Restrictions	NW Forest Pass; trail will likely to reopen to bikes in 2003 for use on odd-numbered days during the summer and fall, call for current status
More Info	Mount Baker-Snoqualmie National Forest, Snoqualmie District (North Bend), 425-888-1421, www.fs.fed.us/r6/mbs/

The Middle Fork

Prelude

The Middle Fork of the Snoqualmie River is rugged and beautiful. Cascading creeks and huge ancient trees decorate the banks of this river. During August when the Middle Fork Trail is dry, it is one of the best trails in business—smooth singletrack through old growth. The clay soil tread on the last few miles of this loop can be unridable in wet weather (and even when it seems dry). Luckily, the Forest Service rebuilt that section of trail with lots of stairsteps, gravel, and turnpikes. Just make sure to keep your speed down and respect the hikers and equestrians who also use this trail. After years of bitter fighting between several environmental groups and the mountain bike community, it looks as though the Forest Service will get off the fence in 2003 and finish a plan that will reopen the Middle Fork Trail to bikes. This is not yet certain, so call ahead before you go riding. If it works out, this is great news, even though the trail will only be open to bikes during the summer

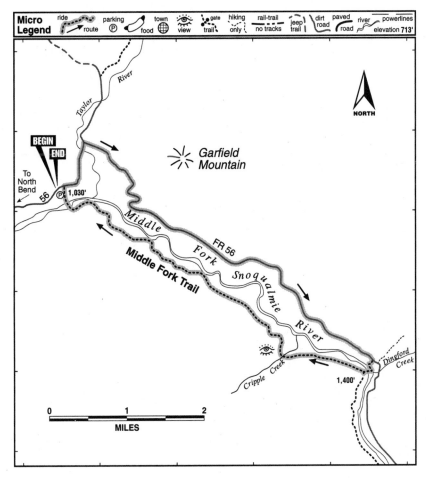

Micro Legend

ride route · parking ℗ · town · food · view · gate / hiking trail only · rail-trail / no tracks · jeep trail · dirt road · paved road · river · powerlines · elevation 713'

and fall on an every-other-day basis. It's not ideal, but that's what we got. Don't poach the trail on even-numbered days because the trail could be closed to bikes again if the Forest Service decides the alternate-days compromise isn't working. In the meantime, just remember there are 32 odd-numbered days in July and August. How many Middle Fork rides do you need in a year?

Driving Directions

From Seattle, take Interstate 90 eastbound to Exit 34. At the end of the exit ramp, set your odometer to zero and turn left on S.E. Edgewick Road. At 0.4 mile, turn right onto S.E. Middle Fork Road (becomes Forest Road 56). Reach a fork at 1.4 miles, and stay right. At 3 miles, the road becomes dirt, and it can be rough from here on out. At 12.4 miles, find the large dirt parking area for the Middle Fork trailhead on the right.

The Ride

From the parking area, ride back out to Middle Fork Road (FR 56) and turn right. After **0.5 mile**, cross a bridge over the Taylor River. At a fork in the road just beyond the bridge, turn right continuing on FR 56. Immediately begin climbing up the western wing of Garfield Mountain on the rocky road. At **1.2 miles**, reach the top of the worst climb of the ride. From here, glide back down to the Middle Fork of the Snoqualmie River. **Whoa**—watch for cars on this descent.

A zippy stretch of trail

At **2.1 miles**, reach the bottom of the hill and veer to the left, pedaling gradually uphill. The road is pockmarked, and there's a second steep climb followed by a short descent. After several more miles of easy climbing, reach the Dingford Creek Trailhead, **6.5 miles**. Find the Middle Fork Trail 1003, which exits the trailhead parking area on the right. The trail drops to the river. **Whoa**—this is a heavily used trail, so walk on this steep section if necessary. At **6.7 miles**, reach a suspension bridge and cross over the Middle Fork of the Snoqualmie River.

When the trail divides at the opposite bank, turn right and ride up the hill. Some walking will be necessary. At the top, **6.9 miles**, bear right to continue down river, ignoring the trail back on the left. Be considerate of this pine-needle trail. Ride downriver on the narrow singletrack through heavy forest. Cross numerous bridges that span tributaries and wetlands. Occasionally the trail travels close to the river, but mostly it hugs the base of the steep mountains. Around **10.0 miles**, the trail is built up with gravel and log stairs. Ride with care and watch for other users. At **12.9 miles**, after 50 yards of rocky exposure, reach a suspension bridge that crosses back over the river. The parking area on the opposite side completes the loop, **13.0 miles**.

NOTES:

_____

_____

Ride 11 ✹✹✹✹

MIDDLE FORK–EXTENDED

Distance	**23.1 miles**, loop
Terrain	Singletrack, dirt roads; long road climb with some steep sections, lots of short hills on the trail, some walking, **cumulative gain: 1,900 ft.**
Duration	4 to 6 hours
Travel	46 miles from Seattle
Skill Level	Expert
Season	Late summer, early fall
Maps	Green Trails *Mount Si, Skykomish, Snoqualmie Pass*
Explorability	Low
Restrictions	NW Forest Pass; trail will likely to reopen to bikes in 2003 for use on odd-numbered days during the summer and fall, call for current status
More Info	Mount Baker-Snoqualmie National Forest, Snoqualmie District (North Bend), 425-888-1421, www.fs.fed.us/r6/mbs/

Prelude

Rugged and majestic, surrounded by stunning rock and wilderness, the Middle Fork of the Snoqualmie River valley is one of the most beautiful areas described in *Kissing the Trail*. This route parallels the Middle Fork up the north bank on a gravel and dirt road and back down the south on a wild conglomerate of a trail that combines whorling 6-inch treads, tightrope-straight logging railroad grades, tricky creek crossings and river fords, and beautiful stretches of old growth. Though it's been closed to bikes for six years, the Middle Fork Trail will likely reopen to bikes in 2003, but only during the summer and early fall and only on an every-other-day basis. Don't poach the trail when it's closed or the Forest Service will close it altogether. Walk to prevent trail damage and walk to yield the way to other users. Since Goldmyer Hotsprings is operated by a private, nonprofit group, reservations and some cash are required if you want to soak in the hot pools at the halfway point. For Goldmyer information, call 206-789-5631.

Cyclist ponders numb feet

Taking a scenic break

Driving Directions

From Seattle, take Interstate 90 eastbound to Exit 34. At the end of the exit ramp, set your odometer to zero and turn left on S.E. Edgewick Road. At 0.4 mile, turn right onto S.E. Middle Fork Road (Forest Road 56). Reach a fork at 1.4 miles, and stay right. At 3 miles, the road becomes dirt, and it can be rough from here on out. At 12.4 miles, find the large dirt parking area for the Middle Fork trailhead on the right.

The Ride

From the parking area, ride out to Middle Fork Road (FR 56) and turn right. After **0.5 mile**, cross a bridge over the Taylor River (see Ride 13). At a fork in the road just beyond the bridge, take a hard right to continue on FR 56. Immediately begin climbing the rocky road. At **1.2 miles**, reach the top, then glide back down to the Middle Fork of the Snoqualmie River. **Whoa**—watch for vehicles on the road during this descent.

At **2.1 miles**, reach the bottom of the hill. The road bends to the left, gradually angling uphill. After several miles of easy climbing with one tough hill thrown in for good measure, pass the Dingford Creek Trailhead, **6.5 miles** (see Ride 10). Continue up the dirt road. Just around the corner from the parking area, pass over Dingford Creek, with Dingford Falls on the left. The falls are a nice place for a breather and an energy bar.

The road keeps up a steady climb from Dingford. At **10.1 miles**, ignore a road on the right that heads down toward the river. At **11.1 miles**, the road forks. Take the lesser road on the right that drops to the river, **11.3 miles**. Ford the river, and find the trail on the opposite bank. **Whoa**—use extreme care when crossing the river, as the icy water numbs feet in about 28 nanoseconds. Just across the river, reach a 4-way intersection. (The trail on the left heads upriver; the trail straight ahead leads to the Goldmyer Hotsprings caretaker's cabin, in case you've got the time, money, and res-

Spinning up Forest Road 56

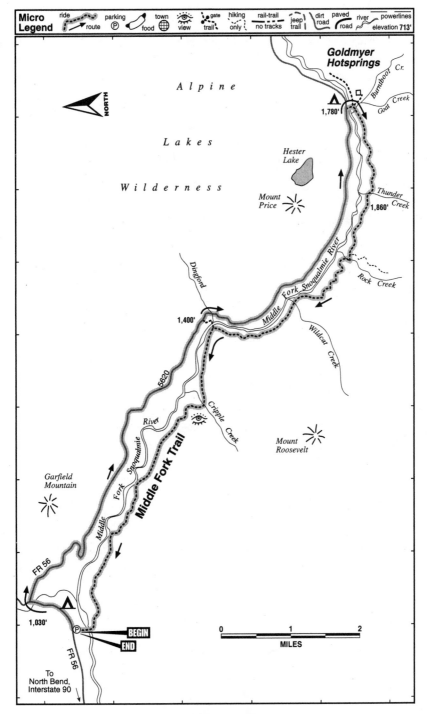

ride
route
parking
P
town
food
view
gate
trail
hiking
only
rail-trail
no tracks
jeep
trail
dirt
road
paved
road
river
powerlines
elevation 713'

NORTH

Goldmyer
Hotsprings

Burntboot Cr.

Goat Creek

Alpine

1,780'

Lakes

Hester
Lake

Thunder
Creek

1,860'

Wilderness

Mount
Price

Middle Fork Snoqualmie River

Dingford

Rock Creek

1,400'

Wildcat Creek

5620

Cripple Creek

River

Mount
Roosevelt

Middle Fork Snoqualmie

Middle Fork Trail

Garfield
Mountain

Middle

FR 56

1,030'

BEGIN

END

P

0   1   2

MILES

FR 56

To
North Bend,
Interstate 90

Middle Fork of the Snoqualmie River   **71**

ervation for a hot soak.) Turn right onto Middle Fork Trail 1003. Follow the main trail. When the trail forks at **11.5 miles**, bear right. Reach a camp area and take take three quick right turns to reach the banks of Burntboot Creek, and another river ford. This is perhaps a more difficult crossing than the previous one, so be careful.

On the opposite bank, locate the Middle Fork Trail, **11.7 miles**. The trail here is faint and not well-maintained, so it may take a minute to find. From Burntboot Creek, the trail is more darting sparrow than gliding hawk—both extremely narrow and unpredictable. Beginning around **12.3 miles**, however, the route follows an old logging railroad grade for almost a mile. It's straight, fast, and a little rocky. Reach

Cyclist awed by a massive cedar

Thunder Creek at **13.0 miles**. While Thunder Creek is not a big river, wet rocks and awkward footing make the crossing treacherous.

Beyond Thunder Creek, the riding is less difficult and parts of the trail route along the railroad grade. Reach a fork, **14.1 miles**, and go right. The trail drops, winds, and then climbs back up to the railroad grade. Cross a creek at **15.5 miles**. At **16.8 miles**, the trail divides. Take the trail on the left that stays high. (The right fork drops to a suspension bridge across the Middle Fork of the Snoqualmie River and then up to Dingford Creek Trailhead for an easier route back.)

Ignore a trail on the right at **16.9 miles**. In dry weather, it seems as though you can glide much of the next mile, through thick forest on narrow singletrack. Cross numerous bridges that span tributaries and wetlands. Occasionally the trail travels close to the river, but mostly it hugs the base of the steep mountains. From the **20.0-mile** mark on, the trail is built up with turnpikes, stairs, and lots of gravel to keep trail users away from the clay soil that turns to peanut butter whenever it's wet. Watch out for others on the trail. At **23.0 miles**, after 50 yards of riding along a cliff above the river, reach a suspension bridge over the river. Cross the bridge and find the parking area on the opposite side to complete the loop, **23.1 miles**.

NOTES:

_____

_____

Ride 12 ✺ ✺

GOLDMYER HOTSPRINGS

Distance	**10.5 miles**, out and back
Terrain	Dirt road; steady climb, sometimes steep, **cumulative gain: 550 ft.**
Duration	2 to 3 hours
Travel	46 miles from Seattle
Skill Level	Intermediate (some sections of rough road, river ford)
Season	Summer, early fall
Maps	Green Trails: *Skykomish, Snoqualmie Pass*
Explorability	Low
Restrictions	NW Forest Pass, reservations required at Goldmyer (206-789-5631)
More Info	Mount Baker-Snoqualmie National Forest, Snoqualmie District (North Bend), 425-888-1421, www.fs.fed.us/r6/mbs/

Prelude

Here's a lovely, relatively easy ride along the Middle Fork of the Snoqualmie River, from Dingford Creek trailhead up to Goldmyer Hotsprings. It's all on a road, but the road is gated. If you want to soak in the hotsprings, call ahead for reservations. And then take care while fording the river.

Parked on the bridge over Dingford Falls

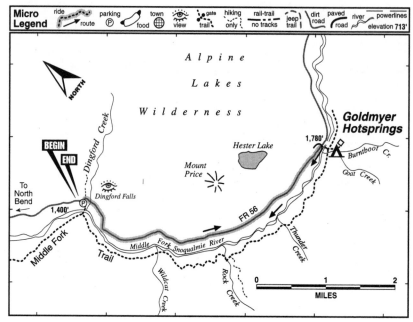

Micro Legend: ride route · parking ℗ · town food ⊕ · view · gate hiking trail · hiking only · rail-trail no tracks · jeep trail · dirt road · paved road · river · powerlines · elevation 713'

Driving Directions

From Seattle, take Interstate 90 eastbound to Exit 34. At the end of the exit ramp, set your odometer to zero and turn left on S.E. Edgewick Road. At 0.4 mile, turn right onto S.E. Middle Fork Road (Forest Road 56). Reach a fork at 1.4 miles, and stay right. At 3 miles, the road becomes dirt, and it can be rough from here on out. At 12.4 miles, pass the Middle Fork trailhead parking on the right. Cross a bridge then, at 13 miles, turn right at the fork to remain on FR 56. The road is very rough from this point on. Park at the Dingford Creek trailhead, 18 miles.

The Ride

From the Dingford Creek Trailhead, ride up the road that parallels the Middle Fork of the Snoqualmie River. Just around the corner from the parking area, pass Dingford Falls. The road climbs gradually with a couple hearty pitches thrown in. At **3.8 miles**, ignore a road on the right. When the road forks again at **4.8 miles**, take the lesser road to the right, and glide down to the river, **5.0 miles**. Ford the river, and find the trail on the opposite bank. Follow the main trail for one quarter-mile, bypassing campsite spurs, to the Goldmyer Hotsprings cabin, **5.25 miles**. When you're done soaking, pedal back to the Dingford Creek trailhead, **10.5 miles**.

NOTES:

Ride 13 ✹✹✹

TAYLOR RIVER

Distance	**13.4 miles**, out and back
Terrain	Dirt trail, dirt road; gradual climb, **cumulative gain: 900 ft.**
Duration	2 to 4 hours
Travel	46 miles from Seattle
Skill Level	Advanced
Season	Summer, early fall
Maps	Green Trails: *Skykomish*, *Mount Si*
Explorability	Low
Restrictions	NW Forest Pass
More Info	Mount Baker-Snoqualmie National Forest, Snoqualmie District (North Bend), 425-888-1421, www.fs.fed.us/r6/mbs/

Prelude

The old road up Taylor River to the Alpine Lakes Wilderness boundary evidences the powers of Mother Nature: A small landslide here, a fickle tributary there, and some fast-growing northwest flora have all but erased the road, making it one of the best road-to-trail conversions I've seen. Though not exactly singletrack, the route looks like a trail much of the way. And chainring-sized rocks and meandering creeks make for a challenging ride, especially in wet conditions. If you bring a day pack, you can stash your bike at the Wilderness boundary and hike up to Snoqualmie Lake, or to Nordrum Lake if you really want a challenge. If the trail is overgrown, practice a little "rolling trail maintenance," by keeping logs and rocks off the tread and shrubs out of your face.

Otter Falls

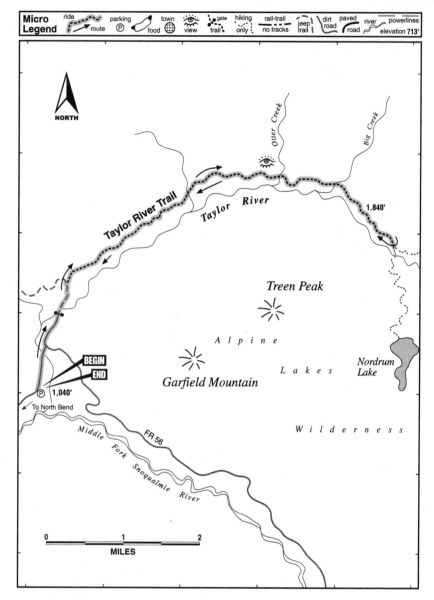

Micro Legend: ride · route · parking ⓟ · town food ⊕ · view · gate trail · hiking only · rail-trail no tracks · jeep trail · dirt road · paved road · river · powerlines · elevation 713'

NORTH

Otter Creek

Big Creek

Taylor River Trail

Taylor River

1,840'

Treen Peak

Alpine

Lakes

Nordrum Lake

Garfield Mountain

BEGIN
END

ⓟ 1,040'

To North Bend

Middle Fork Snoqualmie River

FR 56

Wilderness

0   1   2
MILES

Driving Directions

From Seattle, take Interstate 90 eastbound to Exit 34. At the end of the exit ramp, set your odometer to zero and turn left on S.E. Edgewick Road. At 0.4 mile, turn right onto S.E. Middle Fork Road (Forest Road 56). Reach a fork at 1.4 miles, and stay right. At 3 miles, the road becomes dirt, and it can be rough from here. At 12.4 miles, find the dirt parking area for the Middle Fork trailhead on the right.

The Ride

From the parking area, ride back to the Middle Fork Road (FR 56). Turn right and pedal north. Cross a paved bridge over the Taylor River at **0.5 mile**. When the road forks just beyond the bridge, take the left fork, ascending slightly. The road is gated at the **1.0-mile** mark. Pass around the gate and, for a second time, over the Taylor River.

When the road forks at **1.4 miles**, take the lesser fork to the right. **Whoa**—this is an easy turn to miss. (The left fork climbs up Quartz Creek Road toward Lake Blethen.) The road immediately narrows to a wide singletrack. Large rocks, small washouts, and a gradual incline pose challenges for even skilled riders.

Pass over an old wood bridge, **3.9 miles**. Just beyond, a landslide requires a short walk. At **5.8 miles**, reach the out-of-place paved bridge over Otter Creek. Above, Otter Falls sheets over large rocks. The trail may be overgrown with brush in places—put your helmet down and forge ahead. At **6.7 miles**, arrive at the old trailhead for Snoqualmie and Nordrum Lakes. From here, either put on your hiking boots or turn around and ride back to the car, **13.4 miles**.

NOTES:

_____

_____

_____

_____

Ride 14 ✸ ✸ ✸ ✸ ✸

MIDDLE FORK GRAND TOUR

Distance	**54.6 miles,** loop
Terrain	Singletrack, dirt roads, paved roads; many short- and medium-length climbs, **cumulative gain: 3,700 ft.**
Duration	7 to 12 hours
Travel	35 miles from Seattle
Skill Level	Expert
Season	Summer
Maps	Green Trails: *Bandera, Mount Si, Skykomish*
Explorability	Moderate
Restrictions	Middle Fork Trail will likely to reopen to bikes in 2003 for use on odd-numbered days during the summer and fall, call for current status
More Info	Mount Baker-Snoqualmie National Forest, Snoqualmie District (North Bend), 425-888-1421, www.fs.fed.us/r6/mbs/

Prelude

Some mountain biking power hosses attempt Highway 410's Triple Crown: Crystal Mountain (see Ride 49), Ranger Creek (see Ride 48), and Suntop (see Ride 45) all in one day. Others boldly brave the Grand Railroad Tour (see Ride 65). Well, you can add this charming 55-mile Middle Fork loop to those suffer-a-thons. As described here, this route measures 11 miles farther than the version included in the second edition of *Kissing the Trail*, and those 11 miles make all the difference— whether it's chasing daylight, carrying enough liquids, riding on beautiful trails, or suffering. The Grand Tour of the Middle Fork combines the CCC Road (see Ride 8), the CCC Extension (see Ride 9), and Middle Fork–Extended (see Ride 11), then throws in a long stretch of the Middle Fork Road for good measure. If you feel like burning every last calorie and then some, this is one of your best bets. Be sure to carry extra clothes, plenty of food and water, and a light in case you misjudge the amount of daylight you'll need. Stick an emergency jumbo Snickers bar at the bottom of your pack in the event anti-bonk procedures become necessary. For maximum daylight and dry conditions, I recommend an attempt between mid-July to mid-August. Note: The Middle Fork Trail will likely reopen to bikes in 2003 during the summer and early fall on odd-numbered days. However, this is not certain, so call ahead for current status.

Driving Directions

From Seattle, take Interstate 90 eastbound to Exit 31. At the end of the exit ramp, set your odometer to zero and turn left onto Bendigo Boulevard S. At 0.7 miles, turn right onto North Bend Way. At 2.0 miles, take a left onto S.E. Mount Si Road. Despite the road's bends and twists, stay on the main arterial. At 4.7 miles, pass the Mount Si Trailhead parking area on the left. At 5.9 miles, find a wide bus turnaround at a gated, unmarked road on the left. Park here. If this small area is full (unlikely), park at the Mount Si Trailhead.

The Ride

Do not ride up the gated road (toward Mount Teneriffe). Instead, pedal out the paved road and immediately begin climbing. After **0.25 mile**, the road becomes gravel. After quickly gaining more than 300 feet of elevation, the road levels somewhat, **0.75 mile**. Ignore several lesser spurs off the main road then, at **1.1 miles**, pass around a gate. Stay on the main road as you continue upward.

Woof! Reach a 4-way intersection at the top of the hill, **2.1 miles**. From the crest, you can see Mount Garfield and views of the Middle Fork of the Snoqualmie River valley through the trees. Travel straight through the intersection, continuing on the main road. The road, now a doubletrack, rounds the southern edge of a small plateau as it gradually descends. At **3.0 miles**, the doubletrack forks—go left. Continue on the obvious main route. At **3.7 miles**, bear right at the fork. The plateau gives way to a steep hillside just before a stream crossing, and the doubletrack, now more primitive, traverses the steep slope and enters a darker forest, **4.4 miles**. One mile farther, ride back into an older clearcut.

The trail crosses numerous creeks, some intermittent. At **6.8 miles**, cross a substantial creek. Just past the crossing, the route forks. (The right fork drops down to the Middle Fork Road in slightly more than one mile.) Take the left fork (straight). As the road bends to the left, **7.2 miles**, reach another fork. **Whoa**—take the easy-to-miss right fork, an old grassy jeep trail. Here's where this ride really gets interesting. Since the jeep trail hasn't been used much, young alder and Douglas fir saplings have grown up from the trail's tread. Though mostly ridable (with glasses), this section is in serious need of brushing.

Continue pedaling downward on the rough trail. At **9.5 miles**, reach a huge washout that has obliterated the jeep trail. Walk over the boulders to the trail on the opposite side. At **9.6 miles**, reach a T and turn downhill to the right. Arrive at Middle Fork Road at **10 miles** and turn left. At **10.1 miles**, find the CCC Extension Trail on the left and take it. The well-constructed trail winds and switchbacks up the forested hillside.

At **10.5 miles**, reach a 4-way intersection and go straight, now pedaling along a jeep trail. At **11.1 miles**, the CCC Extension Trail starts up again on the left. Take it. From here, the trail winds through a dark forest, crossing several short bridges along the way. It's a fun section of new trail.

The trail ends at a rocky jeep road at **12.6 miles**. (The Forest Service plans to

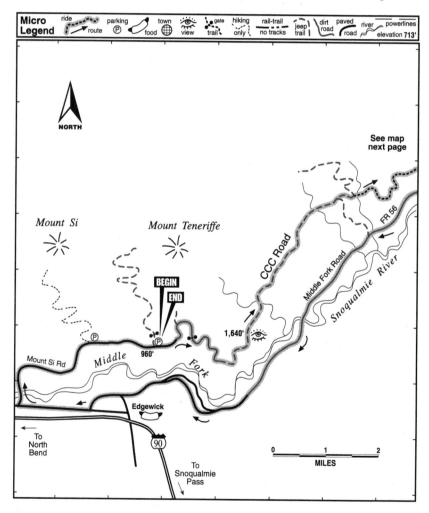

continue the singletrack from here down to the Middle Fork Road near the trailhead, but the construction date is uncertain.) Bear left and descend. Reach a gravel pit at **13.0 miles**. Continue down the road, now dirt, until you arrive at the Middle Fork Road (Forest Road 56), **13.2 miles**. Turn left on FR 56.

Cross a bridge over the Taylor River, **13.4 miles**. Just beyond the bridge, turn right to continue on FR 56. Immediately begin climbing across the western footing of Garfield Mountain. **Woof!** At **14.1 miles**, reach the crest of the climb. At **15.0 miles**, reach the bottom of the hill and veer to the left, pedaling gradually uphill. After several miles of easy climbing and one tough ascent, reach the Dingford Creek trailhead, **19.4 miles**. Just around the corner from the parking area, pass by Dingford Falls on the left.

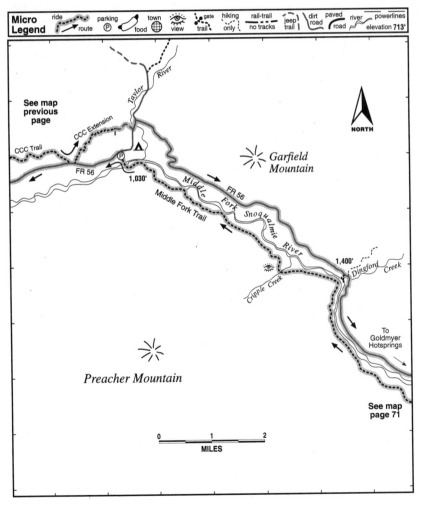

The road climbs steadily from Dingford. At **23.0 miles**, ignore a road on the right. At **24.0 miles**, the road forks. Take the lesser road on the right that drops to the river, **24.2 miles**. Ford the river, and find the trail on the opposite bank. **Whoa**— use caution when crossing the river. Reach a 4-way intersection on the opposite bank— turn right onto Middle Fork Trail 1003. Follow the main trail. When the trail forks at **24.4 miles**, bear right. Reach a camp area and take three quick right turns to reach the banks of Burntboot Creek and another river ford.

Across Burntboot Creek, find the faint, narrow, barely maintained Middle Fork Trail and take it. Beginning around **25.2 miles**, the route follows a narrow, rocky railroad grade for almost a mile. Reach Thunder Creek at **25.9 miles**. It's not a big river, but the wet rocks make for awkward footing. Ride the rolls and swells of the trail to a fork at **27.0 miles**—go right. The trail drops and winds, then climbs back up to the railroad grade. Cross a creek at **28.4 miles**. When the trail splits again at **29.7 miles**, stay to the left.

Ignore a trail back on the right at **29.8 miles**. The next strech of trail is great in dry weather. From the **33-mile** mark on, the trail is built up with turnpikes, stairs, and lots of gravel to keep boots and wheels away from the sticky clay soil. There are more hikers here, so ride with care. At **25.9 miles**, cross a suspension bridge over the river. Reach the Middle Fork trailhead on the opposite bank, **36.0 miles**.

Ride out to Middle Fork Road (FR 56) and turn left. Now pedal to North Bend! Pass the CCC road on the right, **38.3 miles**. Finally, after a very death march, reach pavement, **45.8 miles**. At **46.1 miles**, the road forks—stay high on the left. At **48.4 miles**, the Middle Fork Road ends at a T. (There's food less than one quarter-mile to the left.) Instead, turn right. After a few bends in the road, turn right again on North Bend Way. At **50.9 miles**, turn right on S.E. Mount Si Road. From here, the road winds and climbs (more than you want to know) past the Mount Si Trailhead and back to the parking area, **54.6 miles**.

NOTES:

Ride 15 ✸ ✸ ✸ ✸

WINDY PASS

Distance	**11.5 miles**, lollipop loop
Terrain	Singletrack, dirt roads, jeep trails; long, tough climbs, some walking, **cumulative gain: 2,100 ft.**
Duration	2 to 4 hours
Travel	54 miles from Seattle
Skill Level	Advanced
Season	Summer, early fall
Map	*Ski Acres Mountain Bike Center* map
Explorability	High
Restrictions	None
More Info	Summit at Snoqualmie, 206-236-7277, www.summitatsnoqualmie.com/summer/

Prelude

This ride is demanding both physically and technically. The strenuous climbs and rough trail provide ample opportunity to push those limits. But the wonderful forests and awesome Cascade mountain views make it worthwhile. For cyclists who want even more adventure, there's lots of exploration potential on the many other trails and roads that weave through the area. And a number of new trails have been recently built. This ride does not take advantage of the chairlift that hauls bicycles to the top of the mountain, though this is also an option.

Taking in the Cascades on a blustery day

Driving Directions

From Seattle, take Interstate 90 east to Exit 53 at Snoqualmie Pass. At the end of the interstate ramp, zero out your odometer and turn right. Immediately reach a T and turn left. At 1.4 miles, find the parking lot for Ski Acres Cross-Country and Mountain Bike Center. Park in this lot.

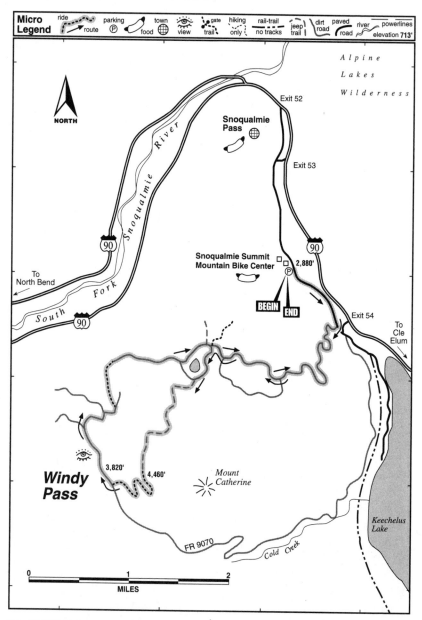

The Ride

From the parking lot, ride back out to the road and turn right. Ride **0.6 mile**, and, just before Hyak, turn right up a steep dirt road. Immediately begin a long and difficult ascent. Spin your granny gear up this steep incline, ignoring spurs, until you reach a large painted wood map of the area at a five-way intersection, **3.1 miles**. This intersection is called Grand Junction.

From Grand Junction, stand facing the map and then proceed down the road to the right. The road bears around to the left then to the right as you pass a lake at **3.4 miles**. At **3.6 miles**, the road forks: Take the left fork up the hill. When the road forks again at **3.9 miles**, take the left fork up a rocky, primitive road. After the short, steep hill, the way becomes more trail than road, but it is still rather wide. At **4.1 miles**, the trail divides—take the left fork onto Trail 18.

From this point, the primitive jeep trail climbs relentlessly, and some walking may be necessary. **Whoa**—there are a few confusing spots—use your best instincts to follow the main trail which becomes a singletrack near the top. **Woof!** Pedal over the crest of Windy Pass at **5.1 miles**. From here the trail switchbacks steeply downward. Due to the erosion potential on this poorly built trail, most of the next quarter-mile should be walked until the trail is re-routed.

At **5.4 miles**, the trail ends in a T. If you turn left, it's a huge descent back to the parking lot; instead, turn right onto the dirt road and climb a short distance to **5.5 miles** where the road crosses the Pacific Crest Trail (PCT). Continue up the main road. When the road divides, **5.6 miles**, take the right fork. At **6.0 miles**, as you pass a pond, again take the right fork, staying on the main road.

Just past the pond, descending now, bypass a road that exits to the right. At **6.3 miles**—descending quickly—ignore a road off to left; at **6.7 miles** again ignore a road to the left. Then at **6.75 miles**, just past a short bridge, the road divides. Take the more primitive left fork. This road, a rocky descent to begin, becomes rough-and-tumble singletrack farther along. At **7.1 miles**, the trail arrives at a rough gravel road next to a power-line tower. At **7.3 miles**, the PCT enters from the right, and for a short way the route is actually along the PCT. During a fast descent, the PCT exits to the left, **7.5 miles**. Continue down the road. Reach a low point and begin ascending. As you climb the hill, stay on the main road. It's a tough climb. At **8.1 miles**, the road tops out and bends right. Reach Grand Junction at **8.4 miles**. From here, retrace your steps down the dirt road and back to the Snoqualmie Summit Cross-Country and Mountain Bike Center at **11.5 miles**.

NOTES:

Ride 16 ⎈⎈⎈⎈

KACHESS RIDGE

Distance	**18.4 miles**, loop
Terrain	Singletrack, dirt roads; long road climb, **cumulative gain: 3,700 ft.**
Duration	4 to 8 hours
Travel	71 miles from Seattle
Skill Level	Advanced
Season	Summer, early fall
Map	Green Trails: *Kachess Lake*
Explorability	Moderate
Restrictions	NW Forest Pass
More Info	Wenatchee National Forest, Cle Elum District, 509-674-4411, www.fs.fed.us/r6/wenatchee/

Prelude

This is one the most beautiful and difficult rides in the book. The high-country meadows on Kachess Ridge burst into bloom in July, and nearby peaks remain snowcapped until late in the summer. But climbing up into this mountain hemlock zone requires some effort, as well as a modicum of route-finding. The first two editions of *Kissing the Trail* recommended a counterclockwise direction, riding up the trail and down the road. Of course, everyone ignored that and rode the loop backwards. So with the third edition, I've finally fallen into step with mountain bike convention and, I admit, good common sense. I've also re-rated it to four wheels. Just take it easy during the descent: Watch out for other trail users and don't skid.

Scree slope near Kachess Ridge

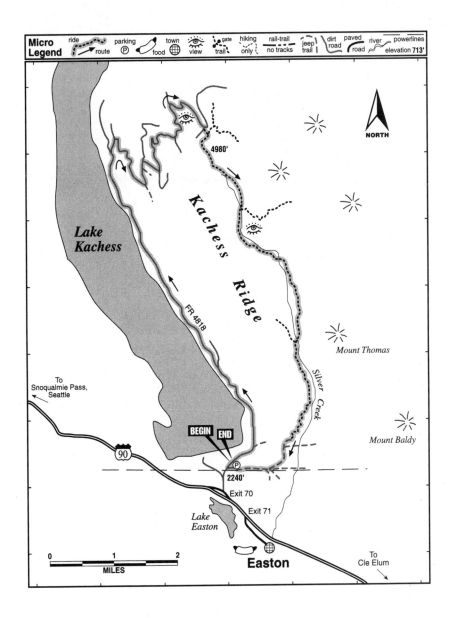

Micro Legend: ride route · parking (P) · town/food · view · gate trail · hiking only · rail-trail no tracks · jeep trail · dirt road · paved road · river · powerlines · elevation 713'

Lake Kachess

4980'

Kachess Ridge

FR 4818

Silver Creek

Mount Thomas

Mount Baldy

To Snoqualmie Pass, Seattle

BEGIN END

90

2240'

Exit 70

Exit 71

Lake Easton

To Cle Elum

Easton

0 1 2
MILES

NORTH

Driving Directions

From Seattle, drive east on Interstate 90 to Exit 70. At the end of the I-90 ramp, set your odometer to zero and turn left. Cross over I-90, then immediately bear left toward Kachess Dam Road. Take the third right turn, 0.7 mile, following the signs to Kachess Ridge Trail. This is Forest Road 4818. At 1.1 miles, park on the right under the power lines.

Road above Kachess Lake

The Ride

From the ad hoc parking, ride away from the power lines along FR 4818. This long stretch of road shoots north above the eastern shore of Lake Kachess. When the road forks at **2.7 miles**, stay to the left along the main road. At **6.0 miles**, reach a fork and turn right. Let the climbing begin! The road divides again at **6.3 miles**—take the right fork.

From here, the road switchbacks up the west flank of Kachess Ridge, climbing over 2,700 feet in less than five miles—a couple pumpkin pies worth of calories. If you haven't been hypnotized by your slowly spinning front wheel, you may notice some nice views into the Alpine Lakes Wilderness to the west and north. Ignore two lesser roads on the right at **7.0 miles** and **7.3 miles**. When the road splits again at **7.5 miles**, however, bear right. Reach another fork at **8.0 miles** and bear left.

If the ascent seems endless, well, maybe you're right. . . At **9.0 miles**, reach a fork and bear left. When the road divides again at **10.0 miles**, go right. **Woof!** The grade finally eases somewhat as you near the crest of the ridge. Remember to check out the panorama of peaks and mountains. Hit a T at **10.7 miles** and turn right. Immediately after this turn, look for a ragged, unmarked trail that drops off the steep embankment on the left. **Whoa**—since this is an unofficial scramble path, it may be difficult to locate. Take the trail on the left.

Follow the trail straight down the bank. At **10.9 miles**, the trail meets up with Trail 1315—turn right. Unfortunately, the climbing's not over: You'll be hike-a-biking or outright pushing for the next one half-mile, up a steep singletrack and across a scree slope. **Woof!** At **11.4 miles**, with jutting rock spires adjacent to the trail and long views up French Cabin Creek valley to the northeast, reach the saddle at the head of Kachess Ridge.

From here, the winding, root-strewn trail descends into a wide, bowl-like valley, which form the headwaters of Silver Creek. The high alpine meadows are delightful, and the views of the craggy peaks to the east are awesome. At **12.4 miles**, reach a fork and bear right. The narrow trail crosses Silver Creek and its tiny tributaries numerous times during the descent. Lower in the valley, however, the swollen creek poses more of a challenge, and a ford is required.

Immediately after fording Silver Creek, **15.1 miles**, reach a fork and bear left. From here, the trail races and whorls down the south face of the ridge. Ride with care, anticipating other trail users and protecting the trail. Pass a small waterfall at **15.8 miles**. When the trail divides at **16.1 miles**, bear left to stay on the main trail. After descending more switchbacks on a loose, sometimes rocky tread, reach the trailhead at **17.1 miles**. From here, ride out the access road. When the road forks at **17.2 miles**, bear right. At **17.7 miles**, reach a 5-way intersection under a set of power lines—bear right and follow the power lines west. At **18.4 miles**, reach the parking area at FR 4818.

NOTES:

_____

_____

_____

_____

Ride 17 ✻✻

HAMLIN PARK

Distance	**1.5 miles**, loop (longer options)
Terrain	Rolling singletrack; **cumulative gain: 200 ft.**
Duration	1 hour
Travel	5 miles from Seattle
Skill Level	Intermediate (beginner singletrack)
Season	Year round (sensitive trail: avoid during wet weather)
Maps	USGS: *Seattle North, Edmonds East*
Explorability	Moderate
Restrictions	Day-use only
More Info	City of Shoreline, 206-546-5041, www.cityofshoreline.com/parks/

Prelude

This great ride, despite its short length, has the dubious distinction of requiring most directions per mile. It should probably be listed as an Other Destination because you should just go out and ride here, and forget about a particular route.

In this maze of forested singletrack, plan to ride a number of loops, varying your route each time. On parts of the trail, large Douglas firs garnished with salal belie the 1950s subdivisions nearby. Hamlin Park gets a lot of use, so be a courteous trail user.

Driving Directions

From Seattle, go north on Interstate 5. Just past Northgate, take Exit 175 to N.E. 145th Street. Turn right on 145th, and set your odometer to zero. At 0.5 mile, turn left on 15th Avenue. N.E. At 1.2 miles, turn right at N.E. 160th Street. At 1.4 miles, reach the paved parking area for Hamlin Park on the left.

Snow at Hamlin Park

The Ride

From the parking lot, ride out N.E. 160th back toward 15th Avenue. After about 100 yards, find the dirt trail on the right. Pedal out the trail to a 4-way intersection, **0.2 mile**—stay on the main trail to the center. At **0.3 mile**, reach another fork; this time turn left. Stay on the main trail to the cement barricades.

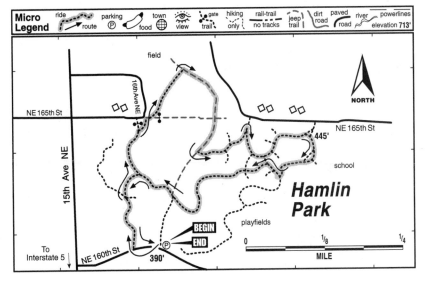

Turn right at the barricades, and then quickly turn left before the second set of barricades (don't go down the hill). Ride straight on what seems like a trail, dropping to a field at **0.45 mile**. Turn right at the field, continuing down a trail.

At **0.5 mile**, pedal straight through a 4-way intersection. About 100 yards farther, take a left, up and away from the wide main trail. Ride up the little gully, passing several lesser trails. Just before the top of the gully, **0.7 mile**, reach a fork and turn right, angling up to the top of a short ridge. At the top, follow the main trail as it bears to the left, ignoring numerous trails that spur off to the right and left. At **0.8 mile**, take the right fork on the main trail. At **0.9 mile**, reach a fork; take a narrow trail to the right, descending vigorously for 50 yards. Beginners may choose to walk this descent. At the bottom of the hill, turn right, away from the fence. When the trail comes to a fork at **1.0 mile**, take a right, walking up a short, rooted hill.

Whoa—at the top you'll discover a maze of trails. From the top, take the fourth left, **1.05 miles**, and then the first right. After a few more pedal strokes, **1.1 miles**, meet a trail and bear left, downhill. Stay on this main trail as it switchbacks once before reaching the bottom to meet up with a very wide trail, **1.2 miles**. Cross this trail and find a trail on the opposite side. Climb away from the wide trail. At **1.25 miles**, find a trail on the left and take it. At **1.35 miles**, the trail forks again: Take the center trail. At **1.45 miles**, reach the paved road. Turn left and ride a short stretch down the hill to parking lot, making the ride **1.5 miles**.

NOTES:

Ride 18 ❀

LOWER WOODLAND PARK

Distance	**4.3 miles**, loop
Terrain	Dirt trails; mostly flat, some rolling hills, **cumulative gain: 100 ft.**
Duration	1 hour
Travel	0 miles from Seattle
Skill Level	Beginner
Season	Year round
Map	City of Seattle
Explorability	Moderate
Restrictions	Bikes not allowed on narrow trails in Lower Woodland Park
More Info	City of Seattle Parks, 206-684-4075, www.cityofseattle.net/parks/

Prelude

Here's a short ride for the beginning rider who senses there might be something beyond the paved path around Green Lake. Despite the weekend throngs and the Lycra-sensibilities of the Green Lake culture, the outer trail around the lake and up into Woodland Park is fun, earthy, and usually not quite as crowded (though you may want to avoid the weekends). This route is open to mountain bicycles, although most of the trails in Lower Woodland Park are not.

Springtime on a wide Woodlawn Park Trail

Driving Directions

Pedal or drive to Green Lake, in north Seattle (near Exit 170 off Interstate 5). Travel south on E. Greenlake Way to the south end of the lake. At 55th Street, turn right onto a parking area adjacent to the Lower Woodland Park playfields and track.

The Ride

Beginning from the Lower Woodland Park playfields, ride south along the wide path that parallels Greenlake Way N. At N. 50th Street, turn right and ride up the hill. Pass tennis courts on your right. Just before

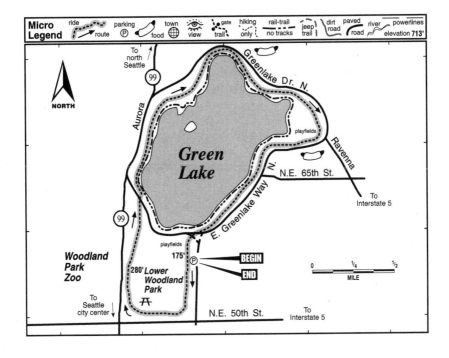

Micro Legend

ride · route | parking · P | town · food | view | gate · trail | hiking trail only | rail-trail · no tracks | jeep trail | dirt road | paved road | river | powerlines · elevation 713'

To north Seattle

99

NORTH

Aurora

Greenlake Dr. N.

Green Lake

playfields

Ravenna

E. Greenlake Way N.

N.E. 65th St.

To Interstate 5

99

playfields

175'

P

Woodland Park Zoo

280' Lower Woodland Park

BEGIN

END

To Seattle city center

N.E. 50th St.

To Interstate 5

0 · ¼ · ½ · MILE

the tunnel, **0.6 mile**, bear right into the gravel parking area. Ride catty-corner across the parking area to the grass, and ride up to the top of the hill, **0.7 mile**. From here, ride north along the roller-coaster path that parallels Aurora Avenue N. From the top of the third hill, **0.9 mile**, continue north on the trail (not the dirt road). Pass behind the restrooms before reaching a paved parking lot. Ride through the parking lot, past the lawn bowling on the right. When you reach Whitman Place N. at the end of the parking lot, turn right. Immediately turn right again onto N. 63rd Street. Green Lake is now across W. Greenlake Way N. Cross the street and turn left on the dirt trail that circumnavigates the outside edge of Green Lake. At **1.3 miles**, the trail runs next to Aurora Avenue for about one half-mile then bends away. Stay on the outside path. At **3.0 miles**, pass the Green Lake branch of the Seattle Public Library on the left. Bear away from the lake at **4.2 miles**, and pass a nine-hole golf course on the right. At **4.3 miles**, reach the intersection of E. Greenlake Drive N. and W. Greenlake Drive N. Cross W. Greenlake Drive N. to the parking area.

NOTES:

Destination 19 ✹✹

NORTH SEATAC PARK

Distance	**2 to 5 miles**, loops
Terrain	Wide and narrow dirt trails, paved roads; short hills, some steep
Duration	1 to 2 hours
Travel	11 miles from Seattle
Skill Level	Intermediate
Season	Year round
Map	No useful maps available
Explorability	High
Restrictions	Day-use only
More Info	Seatac Parks, 206-439-9273, www.seatac.wa.gov/park/index.htm

Prelude

In the olden days, North Seatac Park was a bustling neighborhood, but constant airplane noise made it unlivable. Some streets still remain, and dirt trails crisscross the scrubby area, making countless short loops. The key is to cobble together random loops to create an exhilarating, after-work ride (cyclecross nationals have been held here) that's close to home. You can also perfect your jumps and cross-ups at the BMX area. Vehicle break-ins are common in some parking areas here. Rather than park in an empty lot at night, try parking at one of the nearby gas stations.

Driving Directions

Drive south on Interstate 5. Take Exit 154A to Highway 518, following signs toward the airport. Pass by the airport exit, then take the Des Moines Memorial Drive Exit. Zero your odometer as you turn right on Des Moines Memorial Drive S. **Park area 1:** At 0.9 mile, turn right on S. 136th Street, then right again on 18th Avenue S. Park next to the tennis courts. Ride south on 18th Avenue and enter the park at a gate in the fence. **Park area 2:** Continue north on Des Moines Memorial Drive S. to S. 128th Street, 1.4 miles, and turn right. At 1.6 miles, turn right into a large parking area. Ride away from 128th Avenue on wide trails and paved roads until you cross S. 136th Street. Proceed along the fenceline and enter at the gate.

NOTES:

_____

_____

Destination 20 ✹✹✹

SOUTH SEATAC PARK

Distance	**2 to 7 miles**, loops
Terrain	Wide and narrow dirt trails; rolling hills
Duration	1 to 2 hours
Travel	14 miles from Seattle
Skill Level	Intermediate
Season	Year round
Map	No useful maps available
Explorability	High
Restrictions	Day-use only
More Info	Seatac Parks, 206-439-9273, www.seatac.wa.gov/park/index.htm

Prelude

It doesn't take long riding at South Seatac Park before you'll start thinking of yourself as a mountain bike badass. The trails are raw, sandy, zippy, wide open, and dark, and airplanes menace the area with talon-like landing gear as they glide inches over the tree tops looking like gigantic pterodactyls. As in North Seatac Park, countless trails and spurs have spread out across the area, and the key again is to cobble together various loops until you get tired . . . or the batteries in your light go out. Vehicle break-ins are common here, too, and parking at a nearby gas station might help you avoid getting to know your insurance broker any better.

Driving Directions

Drive south on Interstate 5. Take Exit 151 toward 200th Avenue. Set your odometer to zero as the exit ramp becomes 200th Avenue S. heading west. Cross Highway 99. At 0.9 mile, turn left into a dirt parking area. **Whoa**—it's an easy turn to miss. Ride the paved trail a short distance to a singletrack on the right. Have fun.

NOTES:

_____

_____

_____

_____

Ride 21 ✦✦

DRUNKEN CHARLIE LAKE

Distance	**8.5 miles**, out and back
Terrain	Dirt roads; some short but very steep hills, **cumulative gain: 950 ft.**
Duration	1 to 2 hours
Travel	33 miles from Seattle
Skill Level	Beginner
Season	Year round
Maps	USGS: *Sultan, Lake Joy*
Explorability	High
Restrictions	None
More Info	Neither King County nor DNR answer recreation questions

Prelude

With 11,000 acres, the Marckworth Forest is one of the largest public forests left in the lowlands of western King County. The forest is owned by King County and

Road to Drunken Charlie Lake

various trusts, but it is managed—and logged—by the Washington State Department of Natural Resources. Because of its vast size and proximity to Puget Sound's urban centers, the Marckworth could become a terrific regional park that would dwarf Cougar Mountain, alleviating pressure for trails and open space. King County and Snohomish County should band together and make this a regional park. Dwindling budgets probably make this idea a pipe dream.

You'll find many miles of gated dirt roads and some trails to explore. The moderate terrain and beautiful, lush forest make this a great ride for beginners; the miles of

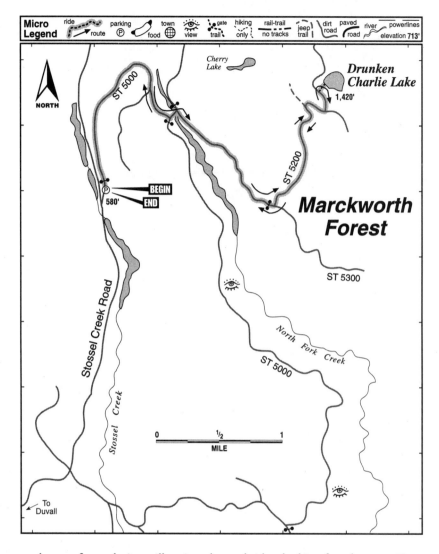

Micro Legend

ride route · parking Ⓟ · town food ⊕ · view · gate trail · hiking only · rail-trail no tracks · jeep trail · dirt road · paved road · river · powerlines · elevation 713'

roads open for exploring will entice advanced riders looking for adventure. Even when riding on gated roads, watch for logging vehicles.

Driving Directions

Take Highway 520 to Redmond. Cross Highway 202, and take Avondale Road to Woodinville–Duvall Road. Turn right, toward Duvall. Reach a T in Duvall and turn left on Highway 203. After several blocks, bear right onto N.E. Cherry Valley Road, and zero out your odometer. At 4.4 miles, bear right as Cherry Valley Road becomes Kelly Road N.E. At 6.9 miles, take a hard left onto N.E. Stossel Creek Way.

Drunken Charlie Lake

At 8.4 miles, reach a fork and turn right onto Stossel Creek Road N.E., which is dirt. Enter Marckworth Forest. At about 9.6 miles, pass straight through a 4-way intersection. At 11.8 miles, take the right fork onto ST 5000 and park immediately.

The Ride

From the fork, pedal up ST 5000. The road gradually ascends through the lush evergreen forests of the Marckworth. After about 100 yards, pass through a white gate and continue up the road. The road climbs easily, then gradually bears to the right. When the way forks at **1.4 miles**, go left and descend for a short distance.

At **1.6 miles**, reach a T. Turn left, immediately crossing over a long narrow swamp. At **1.75 miles**, the road forks again. This time, take a hard right onto ST 5300. From here, stay on the main road, ignoring spurs. The road gradually ascends, paralleling the narrow swamp, which is below on the right. Ride through a small clearcut then after a gate, **2.9 miles**, turn left onto ST 5200.

After the turn, the climb becomes steeper in places. After a short but steep hill at **3.2 miles**, the road forks at **3.9 miles**. Take the right fork, remaining on ST 5200. The road bends right and then climbs steeply again; some walking may be necessary. As the climb levels out, find another fork at **4.1 miles**. Go left, staying on the main road, ST 5200, and continue the climb. At **4.25 miles**, find a vague trail into the woods on the right. **Whoa**—this trail is easy to miss. Less than 100 yards from the road, arrive at Drunken Charlie Lake, a little round lake surrounded by majestic forest. Eat lunch here and then return to the parking area at the start, **8.5 miles**.

NOTES:

_____

_____

_____

_____

Ride 22 ✪ ✪

MARCKWORTH FOREST

Distance	**10.3 miles**, loop
Terrain	Dirt roads; gradual and steep climbs, **cumulative gain: 980 ft.**
Duration	1 to 2 hours
Travel	32 miles from Seattle
Skill Level	Beginner
Season	Year round
Maps	USGS: *Sultan, Lake Joy*
Explorability	High
Restrictions	None
More Info	Neither King County nor DNR answer recreation questions

Prelude

The Marckworth Forest, densely wooded and topographically varied, should be a regional county park (contact the King County Council and State Legislature to voice your opinion). This ride tours dirt roads, mostly gated, in the southeast corner of the forest, affording territorial views of Stossel Creek and its tributaries, and panoramic views of the Cascades and Mount Rainier. The loop passes roads that lead to Drunken Charlie Lake (see Ride 21) and the Tolt Pipeline Trail. Despite its proximity to King County's urban areas, the Marckworth is out there, and there have been problems with recreational shooting, garbage dumping, and crime.

Driving Directions

Take Highway 520 to Redmond. Cross Highway 202, and take Avondale Road to Woodinville–Duvall Road. Turn right, toward Duvall. Reach a T in Duvall and turn left on Highway 203. After several blocks, bear right onto N.E. Cherry Valley Road, and zero out your odometer. At 4.4 miles, bear right as Cherry Valley Road becomes Kelly Road N.E. At 6.9 miles, take a hard left onto N.E. Stossel Creek Way. At 8.4 miles, reach a fork and turn right onto Stossel Creek Road N.E., which is dirt. Enter Marckworth Forest. At about 9.6 miles, reach a 4-way intersection and park immediately.

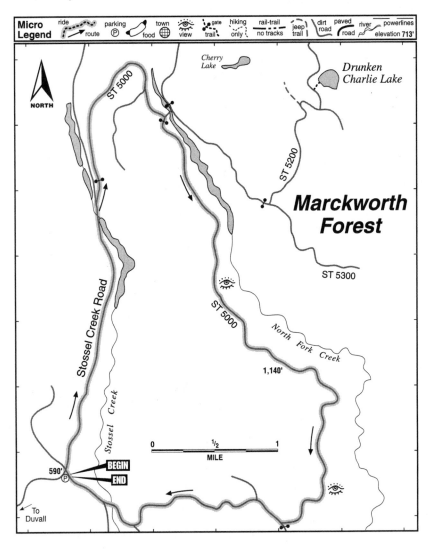

The Ride

From the 4-way intersection, continue out Stossel Creek Road, which is not gated. The road traverses along a high bank above Stossel Creek. Stay on the main road. At **2.25 miles**, the road forks. Go right onto ST 5000, which climbs gradually. After several hundred yards, pass through a gate and continue up. The road forks again at **3.7 miles**— this time go left. Reach a T at **3.9 miles**. (The left fork heads toward Drunken Charlie Lake, see Ride 21.) Turn right, immediately pass through a gate, and begin climbing a short but steep hill.

Over the hill, the road traverses above North Fork Creek, climbing gradually as it heads south. At **5.4 miles**, the Cascades are visible over a clearcut on the left. Continue along the main road. At the **7.4-mile** point, Mount Rainier can be seen ahead. From here, the road descends quickly. During a particularly steep drop, pass a gated road on the left, **8.3 miles**. (This road, which heads onto Weyerhaeuser land, leads to the Tolt Pipeline Trail.)

At the bottom of the hill, **8.6 miles**, take the left fork and begin climbing. At the top, **9 miles**,

Near North Creek on Road ST 5000

stay on the main road to the right. Drop again, steeper this time, to the **9.9-mile** mark. From here, the road gradually climbs to a fork. Take the right fork and continue up the main road. After a short climb, pass through a gate and reach the 4-way intersection to complete the ride, **10.3 miles**.

NOTES:

_____

_____

_____

_____

Ride 23 ✸✸✸

PARADISE VALLEY

Distance	**6.3 miles,** loop
Terrain	Wide and narrow trails; some short hills, **cumulative gain: 450 ft.**
Duration	2 hours
Travel	23 miles from Seattle
Skill Level	Intermediate to advanced
Season	Year round
Map	USGS: *Maltby*
Explorability	Extreme
Restrictions	Day-use only, dogs on leash
More Info	Snohomish County, 425-388-6600, www.co.snohomish.wa.us/parks/

Prelude

With wide trails and narrow, bomber sections followed by one-mile-per-hour U-turn-a-thons, more intersections than odometer clicks, plus some stunts thrown in for good measure, Paradise Valley has something in common with Baskin and Robbins and satellite television—lots and lots and lots of choices. And lots of ways to get lost (just think of it as exploring . . .) Pay attention to the marker trails and intersections I have noted. Snohomish County recently acquired this property and plans to improve it. This probably means a new parking area (stay tuned) and more trail users. Note: It's not all public park land. Some trails on private land may disappear as the parcels get developed, logged, or sold off. Meanwhile, more trails seem to appear, and they all seem like, well, mountain bike trails.

Driving Directions

From Bellevue, drive north on Interstate 405. Near Bothell, take Highway 522 north toward Monroe. From the turn-off, proceed about 5.5 miles to a stoplight. Set your odometer to zero here, and turn right on Paradise Valley Road. At 1.7 miles, after descending a short hill, find a narrow dirt pull-off on the left.

The Ride

Begin by riding back up the hill toward Hwy 522 along Paradise Valley Road. **Whoa**—the road is narrow and most cars drive too fast, so ride with care. At the crest of the hill, **0.1 mile,** find a trail and open area on the left just beyond several large rocks. From the open area, a wide trail and a narrow trail exit—take the wide trail to the left and pedal away from Paradise Valley Road. The rocky trail, a former road, descends gradually. At **0.4 mile**, ride straight through a confusing open area, bending slightly to the left while ignoring several trails on the right and one beyond the dirt pit on the left.

From here, the trail narrows and tilts upward. At **0.5 mile**, reach a fork and bear right. Over the next one quarter-mile, ignore a faint trail on the right and two wide trails on the left. When the trail forks again at **0.8 mile**, go right. Ride through an interesting corridor of young trees and thick brush. At **1.0 mile**, reach a T and turn right. Lots of roots and a little confusion (get used to it) confront you at **1.1 miles**: It's a 4-way and you want to go straight. At **1.2 miles**, pass straight through a more well-defined 4-way, then immediately reach a T—turn right. Stay to the right at forks at **1.25 miles** and **1.4 miles**. Reach a T at **1.5 miles**, turn right again, and drop. As you descend, ignore two trails on the right.

At **1.7 miles**, reach a T at Mainline Trail and turn left. Stay on Mainline Trail, a marker trail which is wide and often muddy, bypassing one trail on the left then three quick trails on the right. When you arrive at the next fork at **2.0 miles**, turn right and climb a narrower singletrack away from Mainline Trail. Stay on the main trail as you climb, passing a trail on the left then a trail on the right. The trail divides at **2.2 miles**— bear right. The singletrack narrows fur- *Getting it on at Paradise* ther, and the faster riding up to this point gives way to slower twisties. At **2.3 miles**, reach a fork and turn left. The trail forks again at **2.4 miles**; this time bear right. At **2.6 miles**, reach a T and turn right.

Whoa—immediately turn right again on an easily missed singletrack. Reach a T a few pedal strokes farther and turn right again. Ignore a trail on the right at **2.8 miles**. Arrive at a T at **2.9 miles** and turn right. At **3.0 miles**, reach a fork and bear left. Almost immediately, turn left on the tight, meandering Fern Trail. At **3.2 miles**, reach a T and turn left again.

Take a break here to clear your head because, believe it or not, the route gets quite a bit more complicated, and the concentric corkscrewing loops might make you lose your way, as well as your mind. Starting again, ignore two trails in rapid succession on the left. Reach a 4-way at **3.4 miles**, and bear left. The trail quickly forks—go left; when it forks again—go right. At **3.6 miles**, pedal straight through a 4-way. The way is more technical here, up and down, around and around, and lots of fun.

Whoa—at **4.1 miles**, reach an important 5-way marker intersection of narrow trails. There's a small stump in the middle of this confluence of trails, and it'll be useful to recognize it if you ever return. From the 5-way, take a gentle left and begin

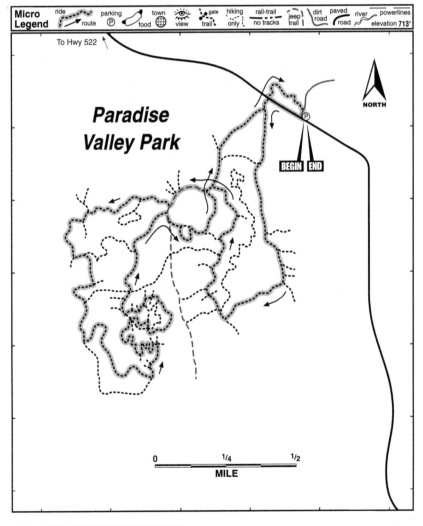

a nutty series of short squigglies. At **4.3 miles**, reach a 4-way and turn right. Almost immediately, ride straight through another 4-way. The trail winds through an open, salal-strewn area to a T at **4.5 miles**—turn right. In quick succession, reach a 4-way and turn left, then reach a T and go left again. At **4.55 miles**, reach a T and turn right. After a few pedal rotations, ignore the trail on the left. Almost immediately, arrive at another fork—bear left. At **4.6 miles**, reach a fork and turn left again. Reach a T and turn right. (Note: A left turn here returns you to the 5-way marker intersection, just in case you want to do the loop, or some variation, again.) When the trail divides at **4.65 miles**, go right and descend, leaving the chaotic but superfun twisties of the Plateau area behind. Ignore a trail back on the left at **4.7 miles**.

One more Paradise amenity

Okay, it's out of the rat maze (we're all rats). Arrive at a 4-way, **4.75 miles**, and pedal straight across the wide, lowland trail to the singletrack that cuts up the bank. It's a healthy climb, though not steep or long. When the trail forks at **4.9 miles**, bear right and follow the rolls and swells of the minor ridge before dropping abruptly. At **5.2 miles**, hit a T at Mainline Trail and turn right. A few rotations of your cranks farther, reach a fork and bear left, leaving the wide Mainline Trail. At **5.3 miles**, turn right at the fork and ride a short gratuitous loop. At **5.4 miles**, reach a T and turn right. When you find another fork, which is almost immediately, turn left on Salal Trail, and noodle along the narrow trail.

Reach Mainline Trail again at **5.6 miles**, and turn right. At the next fork, **5.7 miles**, stay to the left. Ignore a faint trail on the right soon after. When the trail divides at **5.8 miles**, bear left. Reach another fork at **5.85 miles**, and bear right. Arrive at the open area next to Paradise Valley Road. Rather than zip down the road to your car, find the singletrack on the opposite side and take it. Follow the main trail as it drops steeply. At **6.2 miles**, reach a fork and bear right. The trail ends almost immediately at dirt road—turn right. Reach the parking area along Paradise Valley Road at **6.3 miles**.

NOTES:

_____

_____

_____

_____

Ride 24 ✦ ✦ ✦

LORD HILL PARK

Distance	**5.9 miles**, loop
Terrain	Wide dirt trails; easy to moderate climbs, **cumulative gain: 550 ft.**
Duration	1 to 2 hours
Travel	33 miles from Seattle
Skill Level	Easy intermediate
Season	Year round (avoid in wet weather)
Map	Snohomish County Parks: Lord Hill Park brochure
Explorability	Moderate
Restrictions	Day-use only, dogs on leash
More Info	Snohomish County, 425-388-6600, www.co.snohomish.wa.us/parks/

Prelude

A terrific battle of geographical place names is being fought in Snohomish County at Lord Hill Regional Park. Devils Butte, the park's significant geographical feature, quietly dominates much of the site. But even a century after homesteader Mitchell Lord's death, his name still headlines the park. Hard to believe that the two competing names are a coincidence. The trails in this park are primarily gated jeep trails, wide and muddy October through May. The roughly five miles of singletrack at Lord Hill are not exactly angelic—some sections are hiker-only, others are covered with roots and pockmarked by horse hooves—but intermediate riders should have fun with it. Most of the riding is quite easy, making it a good place for a quick spin if not much for skill building (except for evasive maneuvers around billiard balls of horse pucky). The park gets a fair amount of use, especially by equestrians, so watch out for other users. Slow down to walking speed and talk to the horses and riders as you pass. On the narrow trails, stop your bike to let them go by. This loop passes through second-growth forest and around several lakes. On clear days, you can see both Mount Baker and Mount Rainier.

Driving Directions

Drive north on Interstate 405. Near Bothell, take Highway 522 north toward Monroe. Take the first Monroe exit, W. Main Street, at milepost 23. Zero out your odometer at the end of the ramp, and proceed around the roundabout until you go under the highway. This is the Old Snohomish-Monroe Highway. At 3.9 miles, turn left onto 127th Avenue S.E. toward Lord Hill Park. At 5.6 miles, turn left to enter Lord Hill Regional Park. Park in the gravel lot on the left.

The Ride

From the parking area take the wide, wood-chip trail that exits past the kiosk. The trail drops quickly for the first one quarter-mile. Control your speed to avoid conflicts

Temple Pond

with the many equestrians who use this park. The trail levels and crosses a series of low bridges over a wetlands area. Ignore two spurs on the right that lead to private property. At **0.4 mile**, reach a T. Turn right and immediately ascend a short hill. Turn right at the top of the hill and spin along the wide trail.

There's a fork at **0.8 mile**—bear right and begin climbing again. At **1.3 miles**, bear left at the fork. At **1.4 miles**, take the left fork. A few pedal strokes farther, reach the top of Devils Butte and a lookout over the Snohomish River. On a clear day you can see Mount Baker to the north. From here, turn right to take Loop Trail, a very fun but all-too-short singletrack. At **1.6 miles**, the trail becomes a road, then at **1.7 miles**, reach a T and turn left. When the road forks at **1.8 miles**, bear right, returning to the junction at 0.8 mile. Keep your speed down if you pass other trail users. Turn right at the fork, **2.3 miles** in total, riding away from the trailhead.

At **2.4 miles**, take a right at the 4-way intersection. The route descends then climbs. At **2.9 miles**, find the Pipeline Cutoff Trail—a singletrack—on the left. **Whoa**—this is easy to miss. This trail traverses upward along a hillside. Ignore a trail on the right at **3.1 miles**. The trail ends at the Pipeline Trail, a wide dirt road, **3.3 miles**. Turn left and ride slightly uphill. Ignore an unmarked singletrack on the right at **3.3 miles**. Reach a 4-way intersection at **3.6 miles** and turn right onto Temple Pond Loop. This trail, a wide singletrack, descends toward Temple Pond. Ignore a singletrack on the right at **3.7 miles**. A short distance farther, the trail braids apart then reconnects. Bypass a trail on the left at **3.9 miles**. Pass by Temple Pond on the right, **4.0 miles**.

Soon after, the trail veers to the left away from the pond then divides—bear to the right on the main trail. From here, the trail winds through the woods, climbing slightly. Stay on the main trail here. At **4.8 miles**, reach the Pipeline Trail again at a 4-way intersection—turn right. Drop headlong down the road for a short distance. Cross two small creeks that originate from Beaver Lake, which is nearby

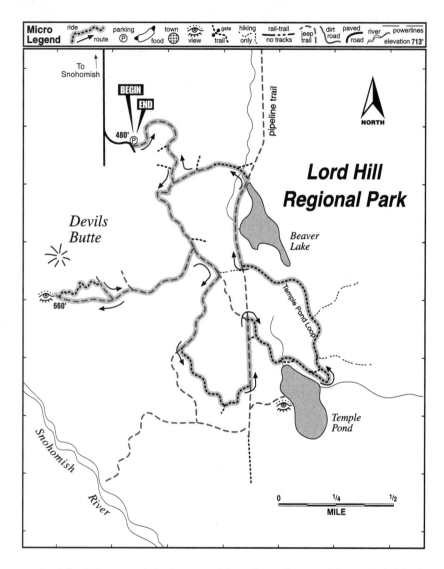

To Snohomish

BEGIN
END

480' ℗

Devils Butte

660'

Lord Hill Regional Park

pipeline trail

NORTH

Beaver Lake

Temple Pond Loop

Temple Pond

Snohomish River

0   ¼   ½
MILE

on the right. **Whoa**—at **5.1 miles**, turn left on the easily missed Beaver Lake Trail. At **5.2 miles**, ignore a trail back on the right. Stay on the main trail as it becomes quite wide. Arrive at a fork, **5.5 miles**, and turn right. From here, follow the trail over the low bridges and back to the parking area at **5.9 miles**.

NOTES:

_____

_____

Ride 25 ✿✿✿

WALLACE FALLS STATE PARK

Distance	**18.4 miles**, out and back
Terrain	Dirt trails, dirt roads; long steady climb, **cumulative gain: 2,650 ft.**
Duration	3 to 5 hours
Travel	44 miles from Seattle
Skill Level	Beginner
Season	Spring, summer, fall
Map	Green Trails: *Index 142*
Explorability	Moderate
Restrictions	State Parks vehicle fee, parking lot closed Mondays and Tuesdays from October through March
More Info	Washington State Parks, 800-233-0321, www.parks.wa.gov

Prelude

The ride up the rail-trail and dirt roads, through mossy forests and fireweed clearcuts, to Wallace Lake offers several outstanding views of the Skykomish River valley, and a pleasant view of the lake at the top. Though the skill level is rated beginner, a change from previous editions due a series new logging roads between the lake and the falls, the long climb and 18-mile distance still make this a three-wheel ride. The top of Wallace Falls, the ride's turnaround point, is interesting, but you should stow your bike and scramble a short distance down the steep, root-strewn hiking trail to the upper overlook for the really spectacular views.

Driving Directions

From Seattle, drive north on Interstate 405 then northeast on Highway 522 to Monroe. From Monroe, take U.S. Highway 2 eastbound. About 13.5 miles east of Monroe, enter the town of Gold Bar. Just before milepost 28 in Gold Bar, turn left onto First Street and set your odometer to zero. At 0.4 mile, turn right onto May Creek Road. When the road forks at 1.2 miles, bear to the left onto Ley Road, following the signs to Wallace Falls State Park. Cross a small bridge. At a 4-way at 1.6 miles, take the middle route. At 1.8 miles, reach the parking area for Wallace Falls State Park. Note: If the parking area is full, and it often is on summer weekends, you'll need to drive back and park alongside the road—tires off the pavement—on the Gold Bar side of the small bridge.

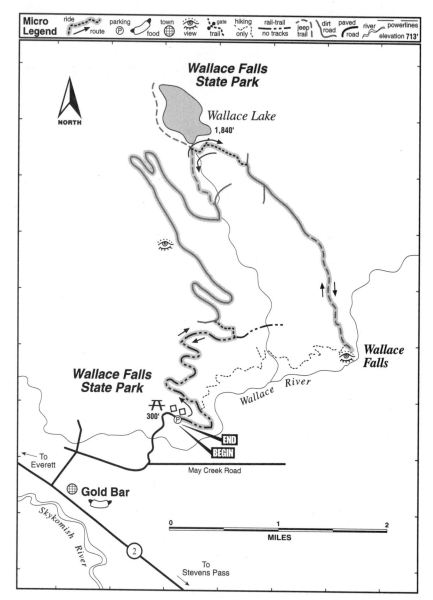

The Ride

From the parking lot, take the wide gravel trail under the power lines. At **0.3 mile**, the trail bears to the left and enters the trees. Pass the hiker-only Woody Trail on the right, **0.4 mile**. The trail, an old logging railroad grade, climbs and switchbacks. At **1.5 miles**, reach a fork at a kiosk—take the narrower left fork and continue the ascent.

The trail ends at a dirt road at **2.4 miles**. Turn right onto the road and continue the long ascent toward Wallace Lake. Stay on the main road, a doubletrack much of the time, as it traverses and switchbacks upward. Pass by a lesser road on the right, **3.9 miles**, and a lesser road on the left, **4.2 miles**. Stay to the right at a fork at **5.4 miles**. Reach another fork at **6.1 miles**—turn left onto the darker, narrower jeep trail that climbs toward Wallace Lake. **Woof!** The climbing is complete at **6.5 miles**, and the old road drops to the lake.

Peaceful and scenic, Wallace Lake is found at the **6.6-mile** mark at a T in the trail. Turn right and cross the short bridge, following the signs to Wallace Falls (the trail to the left travels to the opposite end of the lake). Just beyond

Wallace Lake (photo by Wallace)

the bridge, **6.7 miles**, stay on the main trail to the right. The trail widens. At **7.1 miles**, meet a road and bear right. When the road forks at **7.3 miles**, go left and descend, following the signs to Wallace Falls. The wide gravelly road turns into a narrow dirt road and enters a dark, second-growth forest at **8.0 miles**. Ignore an old overgrown road back on the left at **8.8 miles**.

The air soon becomes fresh and cool as you near the falls. **Whoa**—at **9.2 miles**, pass a sign: Walk Zone. And walking is a good idea, unless you want to plunge off the cliff into Wallace River. From the Walk Zone, a hiking-only trail accesses a number of spectacular views of the falls. The Walk Zone is your turnaround point—retrace your pedal strokes back to the Wallace Falls State Park trailhead, **18.4 miles**.

NOTES:

_____

_____

_____

_____

Ride 26 ✿✿✿

GOSS LAKE WOODS

Distance	**7.6 miles**, loop
Terrain	Zippy, wide and narrow trails; easy hills, **minimal elevation gain**
Duration	1 to 3 hours
Travel	10 miles from Clinton (Plus a 20-minute ferry from Mukilteo)
Skill Level	Intermediate
Season	Year round
Map	Check www.gosslakewoods.org/map
Explorability	High
Restrictions	Limited parking, stay off private property
More Info	Washington State Department of Natural Resources, South Puget Sound Region, 360-825-1631, www.wa.gov/dnr/

Prelude

The group of folks on Whidbey Island who maintain gosslakewoods.org have been working diligently for a number of years to save Goss Lake Woods (a.k.a. Metcalf Trust lands) from being logged. The coalition of hikers, bikers, and equestrians want to permanently remove this beautiful 600-acre site from the state DNR's active timber harvesting ledger. It's a worthy cause, and you should call your state legislator and tell them. And not only is the site beautiful, but the web of trails is almost too fun for words. Indeed, I have a notebook full of directions and scribbles that formed this loop. The best approach here would be to improvise on this particular route or chuck it altogether in favor of personal explorations. If you repeat a few trails, you can put together a great 12-mile ride with virtually no elevation gain—just fun, swooping singletrack. The trails vary from wide and straight to narrow and twisty. Have fun, but watch out for the dog walkers and equestrians.

Driving Directions

Take the Whidbey Island ferry from Mukilteo to Clinton. As soon as you drive off the ferry deck, zero out your odometer, and head north on Highway 525. At 6.2 miles, turn right on Bayview Road. At 8.0 miles, turn left on Andreason Road. At 8.6 miles, turn right on Lone Lake Road. At 9.2 miles, turn right on Keller Road (Goss Lake Road is to the left). At 9.5 miles, find Edgewood Trail on the left. Park on the left side of the road. Don't park in front of any of the houses across the road.

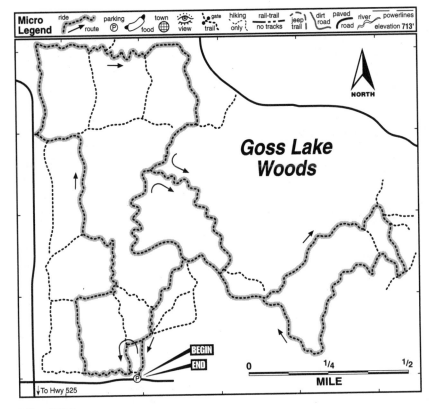

To Hwy 525

The Ride

From Keller Road, head into the forest on Edgewood Trail. Almost immediately, ride straight through a 4-way. At **0.1 mile**, reach a T at the area's map box. This is a handy junction to remember. Turn left at the map box on Frog Lane. Accelerate, click up a few gears, then reach a T and turn left on Ross Road, which is just as wide and straight as its name indicates. At **0.25 mile**, reach a 4-way and turn right on Two Kitties. When you arrive at a 4-way at **0.4 mile**, turn right again on Pete's Path, another wide straight shot through the mixed forest. Reach a T at **0.6 mile** and turn right. At **0.7 mile**, reach a fork and bear left on Coyote.

From here, the trail immediately narrows, winding and twisting. When the trail divides at **0.8 miles**, bear left. Reach a T at **0.9 mile** and turn left. At a fork, **1.0 mile**, go right on Carter Berry Trail, which is wider, faster, and less technical. Reach a T at **1.4 miles**, and turn left. Arrive at a 4-way just before a small parking area off Lone Lake Road at **1.5 miles**—turn right. The trail narrows again as it shoots north. Ignore a trail on the left at **1.8 miles**.

When you reach a fork at **2.0 miles**, turn left onto Blazing Saddles, a very technical trail. (Check the map for an easier ride-around.) Though Blazing Saddles

On the bucking Blazing Saddles Trail

is the most technical trail included in this route, it's less than one quarter-mile long. At **2.1 miles**, reach a fork and bear right. After lots of ups and overs and tight turns in and out of the wrinkles of the forest floor, reach a T at **2.2 miles**—turn left, this is Roller Coaster. After a short distance, the trail bends to the west, then elbows again to the south. At **2.7 miles**, reach a T and go right. When the trail divides at **2.8 miles**, take the left channel. The two channels flow back together a short distance farther—bear left at the confluence.

At **2.9 miles**, reach a fork and bear left on Flying Squirrel (a.k.a Pteromys). The next half-mile is one of the best at Metcalf Trust, winding and semi-technical through an open, second-growth forest (and that's why you're going to ride it twice). When the trail forks at **3.5 miles**, bear right (ignoring Sleepy Hollow). A few pedal strokes farther, reach a T and turn right. Around the **3.6-mile** mark, ignore two trails in quick succession on the left. When the trail forks at **3.9 miles**, bear right. It's a bit technical here, so keep your eyes on the trail. You've completed a loop when you reach the fork at **4.3 miles**—turn right and ride the zippy branch-hopping of Flying Squirrel once more.

Bypass Sleepy Hollow again at **4.8 miles**. Immediately hit a T and turn left. Ignore two private trails on the right at **4.9 miles**. The trail splits at **5.0 miles**—stay to the right. Ignore a trail on the right at **5.4 miles**. Glide up to a T at **5.5 miles**—go left on a wide trail. Next comes a fast series of right turns, one at **5.6 miles** and three at **5.7 miles**. At **5.8 miles**, reach a fork and bear left. A few pedal strokes farther, ignore a trail on the left. When the trail divides at **5.9 miles**, bear left on the south leg of Saratoga Loop and get ready for a herky-jerky ride.

Hit a T at **6.4 miles**, and turn right. When the trail forks at **6.5 miles**, bear right. Reach a T at **6.7 miles**, and turn left. At **6.9 miles**, arrive at a fork and bear left on Spider Web. At **7.1 miles**, turn right at the fork and then immediately bear left to follow the web. But when the trail divides again at **7.3 miles**, you are in Dickens Land on the Oliver Twist Trail. It's short-lived, however, and when you reach a 4-way at **7.4 miles**, go right. Return to the trail divide at the map box at **7.5 miles** and turn left. At **7.6 miles**, the trail ends at Keller Road.

NOTES:

Ride 27 ✖✖✖

FORT EBEY STATE PARK

Distance	**6.9 miles**, loop
Terrain	Singletrack and wide trails; many, many short hills
Duration	2 to 4 hours
Travel	27 miles from Clinton (plus a 20-minute ferry from Mukilteo)
Skill Level	Intermediate
Season	Year round
Map	USGS: *Port Townsend North*
Explorability	High
Restrictions	State Parks vehicle fee
More Info	Washington State Parks, 800-233-0321, www.parks.wa.gov

Prelude

The maze of zippy trails at Fort Ebey is superfun. They are dry, too, so you can ride there most of the year. This route tours the park's trails, but like Goss Lake Woods (see Ride 26) you may want to chuck this loop in favor of get-lost exploring.

Driving Directions

From the ferry dock in Clinton, head north on Highway 525. After about 20 miles, Hwy 525 becomes Hwy 20—continue north on the main road. About 5 miles farther, just past milepost 25, turn left on Libbey Road, and set your odometer to zero. At 0.9 mile, turn left on Hill Valley Drive. When the road divides at 1.6 miles, turn right and immediately park alongside the road just beyond the gate.

High view of the Strait of Juan De Fuca

The Ride

Start from the double gates at the road junction. Pigeon Ridge Trail begins from the opposite side of the intersection and, as its name implies, begins climbing. At **0.3 mile**, reach a fork and bear left on Fisher Ridge Trail. The trail emerges under a set of power lines. Cross under the power lines, turn right, then immediately turn left, heading back into the woods. As soon as you look up, you'll be at a fork in the trail—bear right on Emilie's Trail. After a rolling traverse across a steep side slope, the narrow trail corkscrews down the bank and into a swale.

Switchback up from the low point, then drop again to a fork at **0.9 mile**. Turn left, then immediately turn left again, ascending Hugh's Delight. Ignore a trail on

Sweet Ebey singletrack

the right near the top. At **1.1 miles**, reach a fork and go right. When the trail divides at **1.2 miles**, go left. At **1.3 miles**, ignore a trail on the left. Reach a 4-way at **1.4 miles**—continue straight, then immediately turn left on Chutes Trail. Arrive at a second 4-way at **1.5 miles**. This time, take a hard right turn and start climbing up Ladders. When the trail divides during the climb, bear right.

At **1.8 miles**, reach a funky 4-way. You want to take the middle route, but to do this requires a left then a quick right onto High Traverse. Bypass a trail on the right at **2.0 miles**. Ignore a trail on the left, then ignore another trail on the right as you descend. At a 4-way, **2.3 miles**, turn left then immediately right to get onto Alder Grove Trail. Ignore a trail on the right. Then at **2.5 miles**, turn right onto Humpty Dump (that's the name, okay?). **Whoa**—this turn is easily missed. Bypass a trail back on the left at **2.7 miles** and climb the doubletrack. **Whoa**—don't get too comfortable because at **2.8 miles** you need to take a hard left onto a tasty singletrack, the Roy Evans Trail. This is nice riding.

When the trail splits at **3.0 miles**, bear left. When it forks again at **3.2 miles**, bear left and descend gently to a dirt road. Turn right. At **3.4 miles**, ignore a faint trail on the right. Right away, reach a T and turn left. Ignore the Boundary Trail on the right. At **3.5 miles**, reach a fork and head left. The trail seems to end at a paved road and a kiosk, **3.7 miles**. Bear to the left just before the kiosk, and take Cedar Hollow Trail on a roller-coaster descent. At **4.1 miles**, as the trail bends to the right and begins climbing, you'll find a wonderful view of the Strait of Juan De Fuca from high on the bluff.

From here, the trail switchbacks up the embankment. Ignore the stairs and spur trails to secluded picnic spots as you climb. At **4.3 miles**, reach a fork and bear right. Just after the top, the trail kisses a road—stay left to remain on the trail. Stay on it as it cruises between the group picnic site on the left and the road on the right. Cross

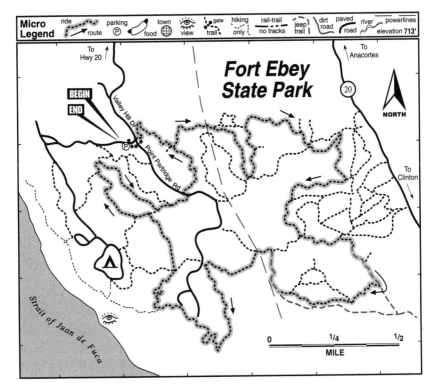

Micro Legend

ride / route   parking ℗   town / food ⊕   view 👁   gate   hiking trail only   rail-trail no tracks   jeep trail   dirt road   paved road   river   powerlines elevation **713'**

To Hwy 20

To Anacortes

Fort Ebey State Park

20

NORTH

BEGIN
END

Valley Hill Dr.

℗

Point Partridge Rd

To Clinton

Strait of Juan de Fuca

0   1/4   1/2
MILE

a road at **4.5 miles**, following the signs toward Fort Ebey. **Whoa**—the trail dances out to the edge of the high bluff. Just beyond, reach a fork and bear right. At **4.8 miles**, reach a fork, go right, and launch down a tight series of technical switchbacks. When the trail divides at **4.9 miles**, bear right on Kettles Trail. Reach a fork at **5.0 miles** and go left on Forest Run.

When you arrive at a T at **5.3 miles**, turn left on Campground Trail. At **5.4 miles**, go right on Hoot In. Reach a fork at **5.7 miles**, and turn right onto Watertower Trail. There's another fork at **5.8 miles**—take a hard right turn on Woodpecker. When you arrive at a T, you've re-joined Campground Trail—turn left and descend. At **6.2 miles**, reach a fork and bear right. From here, it's gradually uphill to a paved road. Turn left on the road, then almost immediately bear right on Pigeon Ridge Trail. Reach a 4-way at **6.6 miles**—go straight by ignoring a trail on the right and then another one on the left. The narrow trail crests a high point then descends back to the paved road and the end of the loop, **6.9 miles**.

NOTES:

_____

_____

Ride 28 ✴✴

SAINT EDWARD STATE PARK

Distance	**2.1 miles**, loop
Terrain	Singletrack; easy rolling hills, **minimal elevation gain**
Duration	1 hour or less
Travel	8 miles from Seattle
Skill Level	Intermediate (beginner singletrack)
Season	Spring, summer, fall (sensitive trail: avoid during wet weather)
Map	*Saint Edward State Park* map
Explorability	Moderate
Restrictions	State Park vehicle fee, day-use only
More Info	Washington State Parks, 360-902-8844, www.parks.wa.gov

Prelude

Saint Edward State Park sits on the lush, forested northeast shore of Lake Washington. The park offers a variety of trails—winding, flat, technical, rolling—so although the ride is short, repeating the trails to add mileage isn't boring. The trails were built and are maintained, in large part, by the Backcountry Bicycle Trails Club. Check out their website if you'd like get involved: www.bbtc.org. By the way, the state parks system, and Saint Edward Park in particular, has worked hard to accommodate mountain bikes, so this is a good place to put in some work. **Whoa**—do not ride on the spur trail that leads down to the lake since many walkers use that trail and accidents could become common. Also, note the new day-use fee.

Driving Directions

From Seattle, take Lake City Way (Highway 522) to Kenmore. Turn right onto 68th Avenue N.E. After a few blocks, 68th Avenue N.E. becomes Juanita Drive N.E. Proceed up Juanita Drive N.E. to Saint Edward State Park on the right. Drive into the park, bear right at the fork, then take the first right into the large parking area.

Saint Edward singletrack

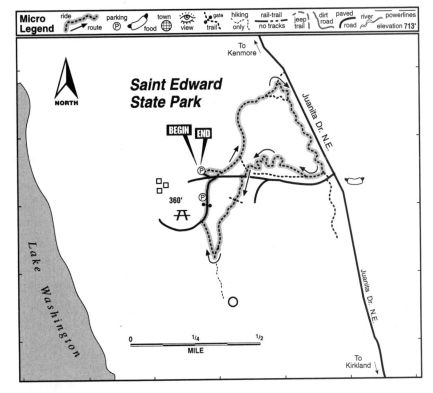

The Ride

Find the trail on the east side of the parking area and take it. At **0.2 mile**, reach a trail junction and bear left. Ride down the wide main trail, bypassing paths on the right and left. At **0.6 mile**, just before Juanita Drive, turn right onto singletrack. When the trail divides after a few pedal strokes, turn left and follow the winding trail to **0.9 mile** (near the park entrance). Turn right before reaching the road. A few wheel rotations farther, the trail forks: Go right. At **1.5 miles**, the trail reaches a T. Turn left and ride 20 yards to the road. Cross the road and find a faint trail that winds through the woods above the playing field. Stay on this trail. At **1.8 miles**, reach a wide, heavily used trail—turn right. Ride down the hill to a parking lot, **2.0 miles**. Continue straight to the entrance road and main parking, **2.1 miles**.

NOTES:

Ride 29 ✺✺✺

BIG FINN HILL

Distance	**4.4 miles**, loop
Terrain	Zippy singletrack; **minimal elevation gain**
Duration	1 to 2 hours
Travel	8 miles from Seattle
Skill Level	Intermediate
Season	Spring, summer, fall (sensitive trail: avoid during wet weather)
Map	*Saint Edward State Park* map
Explorability	Moderate
Restrictions	State Parks vehicle fee, day-use only
More Info	King County Parks, 206-296-4232, www.metrokc.gov/parks/

Prelude

When the City of Redmond closed the watershed, the west section of Big Finn Hill began to get a lot more bicycle use. Why? It's close to where people live, there's nice riding, and there aren't enough other trails open to bicycles. The Backcounty Bicycle Trails Club has done an admirable job maintaining the trails here. Help the BBTC effort. Check out www.bbtc.org to find out about the next trailwork party at Saint Eds. Avoid these trails during wet weather and be courteous to other trail users, and perhaps more King County trails will open to bicyclists. Note: Due to King County budget problems, a local community group is now maintaining Big Finn Hill, and this park may be managed by another jurisdiction in the near future.

Under a tree at Big Finn Hill

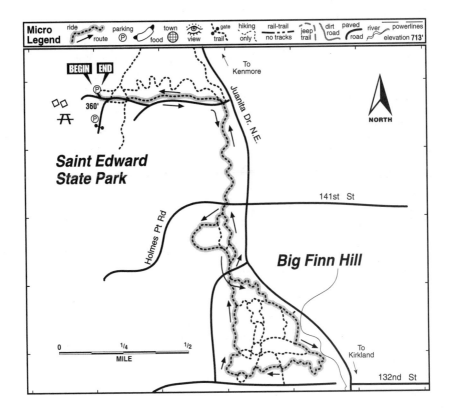

Driving Directions

From Seattle, take Lake City Way (Highway 522) to Kenmore. Turn right onto 68th Avenue N.E. After a few blocks, 68th Avenue N.E. becomes Juanita Drive N.E. Proceed up Juanita Drive N.E. to Saint Edward State Park on the right. Drive into the park, bear right at the fork, then take the first right into a large parking area.

The Ride

From the parking area, ride back toward the park's entrance. Find a narrow paved path on the right between the playfield and the road. Ride up this path to a crosswalk. Cross the road and turn right onto the dirt trail that parallels the entrance road on the opposite side. Ride up this trail to an intersection of trails near the junction of the entrance road and Juanita Drive, **0.5 mile**. Cross the entrance road to the trail on the opposite side, and ride south, paralleling Juanita Drive.

From here the trail becomes much more technical, winding up and down and around tight corners. Reach a fork at **0.9 mile**, and bear left on the main trail. Soon afterward, the trail crosses Holmes Point Drive. Use care when crossing this road. Find the trail on the opposite side. Immediately, **1.1 miles**, take two right turns in

Lush forest at Big Finn Hill

rapid succession. **Whoa**—after the second right fork, watch out for the incredibly steep dropoff into a small ravine. Just after cresting the far side of the ravine, reach another fork: Go right. Just beyond, arrive at a T and turn right.

Pass by a trail that cuts back to the left, **1.5 miles**, then, also at **1.5 miles**, reach a crosswalk across a paved street (where N.E. 138th Place becomes 72nd Avenue N.E.). Cross this road to the trail on the opposite side. Immediately the trail forks—take the left fork. After a fun series of tight corners, reach a wooden bench and a fork. Turn left, pedaling downhill, past an access to Juanita Drive, and then up a short pitch. When you reach a fork, **2 miles**, turn left. Quickly pass a trail on the right, ride over a steep bank, and pass a second trail on the right. At **2.2 miles**, ignore a trail on the right as you wind downhill.

Soon the trail climbs again and some walking may be necessary. Reach a T at **2.4 miles** and go right. When the trail forks almost immediately, turn left. After just a few pedal strokes, take a second left. Pass by two trails on the left at **2.5 miles**. At **2.7 miles**, bypass three trails on the right that lead into a maze of trails at the heart of Big Finn Hill (where the keggers are). At a fork, **2.8 miles**, stay to the left on the main trail. At **2.9 miles**, take the left fork and immediately recross 72nd Ave. N.E.

At the fork just after crossing the road, turn right. Reach a T, **3.2 miles**, and turn right. At **3.4 miles**, take the right fork and then cross Holmes Point Road. Bypass a trail on the left, **3.5 miles**. Arrive at the Saint Edward State Park entrance road at **3.9 miles**. Cross the road to the trail, opposite, and take the trail that parallels the road back to the parking area, **4.4 miles**.

NOTES:

_____

_____

_____

_____

Ride 30 ✹✹✹

SAMMAMISH RIVER RAMBLER

Distance	**23.5 miles**, lollipop loop
Terrain	Dirt, gravel, and paved trails; steep hills, **cumulative gain: 1,700 ft.**
Duration	3 to 5 hours
Travel	11 miles from Seattle
Skill Level	Intermediate
Season	Year round
Map	USGS: *Bellevue North*
Explorability	Low
Restrictions	Marymoor parking fee, day-use only
More Info	King County Parks, 206-296-4232, www.metrokc.gov/parks/

Prelude

The Sammamish River Rambler is back, thanks to a rebuilt trail connection. This long ride links Marymoor Park, the Puget Power Trail, the Redmond Watershed (see Ride 31), the Tolt Pipeline Trail, and the Sammamish River Trail. It's a fun tour of the rolling hills north of Redmond and east of the Sammamish Slough. The riding isn't overly technical, but several steep hills, the length, and the exploratory nature of the route make it a challenge.

Driving Directions

From Seattle, travel east on Highway 520 past Bellevue. Take the W. Lake Sammamish Pkwy N.E. exit near Redmond. Turn right at the end of the highway ramp, following the signs to Marymoor Park. Almost immediately, turn left on N.E. Marymoor Way to enter the park.

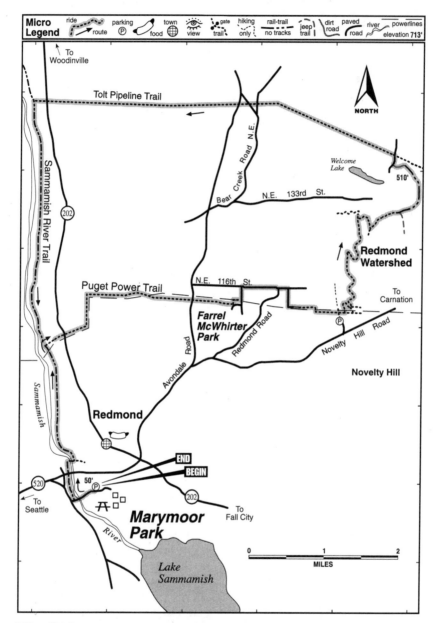

The Ride

From the parking area at Marymoor Park, ride back out toward the park's entrance. Immediately after crossing the Sammamish River, find the paved Sammamish River Trail on the right, take it and ride parallel to W. Lake Sammamish Pkwy. At **0.9 mile**, the trail crosses to the east side of the river—stay on the main trail heading north. Reach a huge set of power lines that crosses over the trail at **2.5 miles**. Just past the power lines, **2.6 miles**, find the Puget Power Trail on the right. Take this dirt and gravel trail, following the signs toward Farrel McWhirter Park. **Whoa**—this is an easy turn to miss, especially after riding along the fast Sammamish River Trail.

The trail ascends a steep hill through the trees, then exits the trees, **2.7 miles**, and follows the power lines. Some walking along this steep section may be necessary. Cross the Redmond-Woodinville Road, then continue the steep climb to **3.1 miles**, where the trail levels somewhat. Just past the **4.2-mile** mark, the trail jogs to the left, becoming a paved bicycle path. When the trail divides at the top of the hill, take the left fork (gravel) that continues under the power lines and descends down to Avondale Road, **5.2 miles**. Cross Avondale Road, then stay left on the main trail toward Farrel McWhirter Park.

Pass over a wooden bridge at **5.6 miles**, and enter the park. Pass straight through a 4-way intersection at **5.7 miles**. Almost immediately, reach a fork and bear left. Then stay to the left as you pass through a parking area. At **5.8 miles**, hit a T under a set of power lines—turn right and climb. When you reach

Singletrack near Redmond Watershed

the top of the hill at **5.9 miles**, turn left on the paved road. (Note: King County is trying to get a soft-surface trail easement between here and the Redmond Watershed, eliminating the need for the next 1.2-mile paved road section.) After a few blocks, turn right on N.E. 116th Street. Pass Redmond Road N.E., then take the next right on 206th Avenue N.E. at **6.8 miles**. Ride this road around the corner to the end, **7.1 miles**, where you'll find a sign: Private Property. No Trespassing. Keep Out. Horses and Bicyclists Okay. Clear as a Tahuya State Forest mud puddle, right? Bottom line, if you're on a bike, you can proceed. Take the wood-chip trail that parallels the private driveway, following the power lines toward a steep hill.

After a short but brutal climb, reach an old fence and turn right onto a singletrack. Continue up the bank on a ragged singletrack next to the fence. At **7.5 miles**, the singletrack joins a wide trail. At **7.7 miles**, reach a 4-way, go straight and keep climbing. When the trail splits at **7.8 miles**, bear right onto a short stretch of singletrack. After a few winds of the singletrack, join the main trail again, and pass

Spinning along the Tolt Pipeline Trail

under the power lines into the woods. The trail, beautiful and winding, swoops downward then ascends to a 4-way at **8.1 miles**—turn left.

From here, follow the wide trail through the Redmond Watershed. It's more produced than the zany Watershed trails of the early 1990s, but it's pleasant and fun. Ignore the hiker-only trails that exit on either side. At **9.7 miles**, reach a fork and turn right on Collin Creek Trail, which is narrower and twisty. Hit a T at **10.1 miles** and turn left. Pass around a mud pit at **10.5 miles**, cross the dirt road, then continue on the trail opposite. Cross a gravel road at **10.8 miles**. At **11.1 miles**, arrive at a gravel road and turn left. A few pedal strokes farther, reach a T and turn right onto the paved road. At **11.5 miles**, the road crosses the wide, gravel Tolt Pipeline Trail—turn left and pedal west.

Follow the extreme tides of the Tolt Pipeline, descending to the lowland ebbs and climbing to the high water mark. Along the way you'll cross numerous driveways and roads. At **13.5 miles**, cross over Bear Creek, a salmon stream in autumn. **Woof!** Ride over the trail's high crest at **15.6 miles**. From here, descend quickly, crossing a new bridge, then cascading down an incredibly steep hill to a busy road at **17.0 miles**. Carefully cross the road, then ride west along the gravel trail. At **17.4 miles**, the Tolt Pipeline Trail ends at a T with the Sammamish Valley Trail—turn left. From here, spin south along the Sammamish River, past Redmond at **22.5 miles**, all the way back to Marymoor Park, **23.5 miles**.

NOTES:

_____

_____

_____

_____

Ride 31 ✹✹

REDMOND WATERSHED

Distance	**5.0 miles**, out and back
Terrain	Wide and narrow dirt trails; easy climbs, **minimal elevation gain**
Duration	1 to 2 hours
Travel	15 miles from Seattle
Skill Level	Beginner
Season	Spring, summer, fall
Map	*Redmond Watershed Preserve* map
Explorability	Low
Restrictions	Bikes not allowed on many trails, day-use only, no dogs
More Info	City of Redmond Parks, 425-556-2300

Prelude

In its heyday, the Redmond Watershed was *the* place to mountain bike because of its zany maze of trails and proximity to Seattle. But even though bicyclists made up about 90 percent of the trail users and the bicycle community offered to build and maintain trails in the park, the city council banned bicycles from the singletrack in the mid-1990s, in large part due to a few selfish neighbors. Well, the trails here have been rebuilt, and while most are still closed to bikes, there is one nice trail through the park. Most of the route follows wide trails, which are more produced than the nutty trails of old, but it's pleasant and beautiful, and the hills are easy. It's perfect for beginners or kids.

Driving Directions

From Seattle, take Highway 520 east to its terminus in Redmond. As Hwy 520 ends, continue straight. Turn right on Avondale Road, and set your odometer to zero. At 1.2 miles, turn right on Novelty Hill Road. At 3.6 miles, find the entrance to the Redmond Watershed Preserve on the left. Turn here and continue to the last parking area.

Fun again in the Watershed

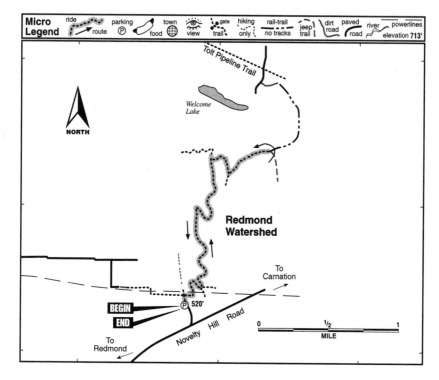

The Ride

The trail exits the parking area in a couple of spots and winds gently downhill to a 4-way at **0.1 mile** under a set of power lines. Turn right here on the wide trail. When the trail divides at **0.2 mile**, bear right onto the singletrack. After a few twists, the singletrack joins the main trail again, and passes under the set of power lines and into the woods. The trail, beautiful and winding, swoops downward then ascends to a 4-way at **0.5 mile**—turn left.

From here, follow the wide trail through the Redmond Watershed. It's much more produced than the Watershed trails of old, but it's pleasant and fun. Ignore the hiker-only trails that exit on either side. At **2.1 miles**, reach a fork and turn right on Collin Creek Trail, which is narrower and somewhat more technical. (You can also explore the trail to the left, but it ends in less than one half-mile.) Reach a T at **2.5 miles** and turn left. Find a mud pit and a dirt road at **2.5 miles**. Turn around here and ride back to the trailhead, **5.0 miles**.

NOTES:

_____

_____

Ride 32 ✿✿✿

TOLT-MACDONALD NORTH

Distance	**4.3 miles**, lollipop loop
Terrain	Dirt trails and jeep trails, sometimes brushy; steep first mile then rolling hills, **cumulative gain: 900 ft.**
Duration	1 to 2 hours
Travel	26 miles from Seattle
Skill Level	Intermediate
Season	Year round
Map	USGS: *Carnation*
Explorability	Extreme
Restrictions	Day-use only
More Info	King County Parks, 206-296-4232, www.metrokc.gov/parks/

Prelude

This old-school Tolt-MacDonald loop begins with a steep, technical singletrack climb from the banks of the Snoqualmie River to the high plateau above Carnation. **Whoa**—the steep embankment up to the plateau slumps on occasion, so creative scrambling may be necessary. From the top, which affords views of the valley and the Cascades beyond, the loop ambles and rolls on singletrack and overgrowth jeep trails. The lushly forested plateau cradles nearby Ames Lake. Once I watched a black bear and two cubs cross the trail here; it was magic. Tread carefully: When we bicycle in the woods, we are in their home.

Town of Carnation from the plateau at Tolt-MacDonald Park

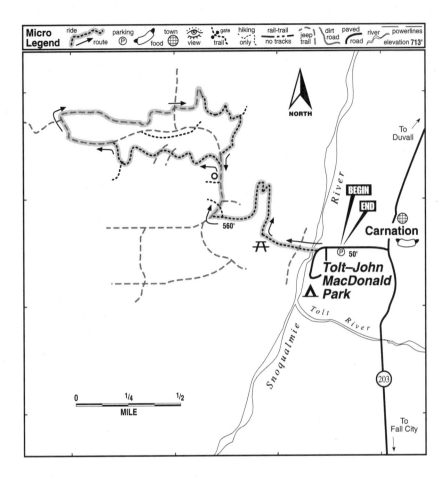

Driving Directions

From Seattle, take Highway 520 east to Redmond. Near the end of Hwy 520, turn right onto Highway 202, the Redmond-Fall City Road. Zero out your odometer here, and head east on Hwy 202. At 7.8 miles, turn left on Tolt Hill Road. After a lot of winding, cross the Snoqualmie River, then reach Highway 203 at 11.0 miles. Turn left on Hwy 203. At 11.5 miles, turn left into Tolt-John MacDonald Park. Drive down the entrance road and park in the gravel lot on the left, 11.8 miles.

The Ride

From the parking area, walk across the suspension bridge over the Snoqualmie River. On the opposite bank, take the gravel road that leads uphill away from the river. At **0.25 mile**, when the gravel road ends, find a trail to the right of the picnic shelter. The trail switchbacks steeply up the hillside, and some sections may have to be walked. Beware the waterbars and any descending yahoos. Just after the trail levels, pass by two trails on the right, **0.8 mile**.

At **0.9 mile**, reach a gravel jeep trail—turn right and continue up the hill, passing several trails on either side. (For trails to the left, see Ride 33.) At the top of the hill, **1.0 mile**, bear to the left.

After the left turn, stay on the wide main path. At **1.1 miles**, pass a big old water tank on the left. Just past the water tank, reach an intersection and turn left. The jeep trails through here are somewhat overgrown: Riding glasses are a necessity. At **1.4 miles**, reach a 4-way intersection—take the center route. Almost immediately, reach a second 4-way intersection and again ride straight through, ignoring the other, wider roads. At **1.7 miles**, at a right-hand bend in the jeep trail, ignore a trail on the left.

Singletrack caravan

Reach a T at **2.1 miles** and turn right. At **2.6 miles**, reach an intersection and continue straight. The trail, a singletrack now, winds and climbs. At **2.8 miles**, reach a fork and bear left. When the trail divides again at **2.9 miles**, go right. Climb to the **3.2-mile** mark, where you'll meet a main jeep trail. Turn left, riding gradually up hill. After passing the watertower (now it's on your right), turn right and head down the steep jeep trail. **Whoa**—at **3.5 miles**, take a sharp left onto the narrow trail that drops back to Tolt-John MacDonald Park, **4.3 miles**.

NOTES:

_____

_____

_____

_____

Ride 33 ✸ ✸ ✸

TOLT-MACDONALD SOUTH

Distance	**8.1 miles**, lollipop loop
Terrain	Technical, user-built singletrack; one long climb then chaotic rolling hills, **cumulative gain: 850 ft.**
Duration	2 to 3 hours
Travel	26 miles from Seattle
Skill Level	Advanced
Season	Year round
Map	USGS: *Carnation*
Explorability	Extreme
Restrictions	Day-use only
More Info	King County, 206-263-6371, www.metrokc.gov/parks/

Prelude

A whole set of great skill-building trails have sprouted up on the plateau above the Snoqualmie River at Tolt-MacDonald Park, and they're all good. Like Ride 32, this ride begins with the same one-mile singletrack grunt up from the river. At the top, however, this route splits off from its Tolt cousin and proceeds along six miles of the most fun, whirling, hepped-up singletrack around. There are many more trails to explore, too. Some of it's technical stuff, especially in wet weather when slippery roots and mud conspire against your equipment and also your will to stay upright. Managed by King County but not by the parks department, the south side of the Tolt-MacDonald plateau has become one of the best riding areas around.

Driving Directions

From Seattle, take Highway 520 east to Redmond. Near the end of Hwy 520, turn right onto Highway 202, the Redmond-Fall City Road. Zero out your odometer here, and head east on Hwy 202. At 7.8 miles, turn left on Tolt Hill Road. After a lot of winding, cross the Snoqualmie River, then reach Highway 203 at 11.0 miles. Turn left on Hwy 203. At 11.5 miles, turn left into Tolt-John MacDonald Park. Drive down the entrance road and park in the gravel lot on the left, 11.8 miles.

The Ride

From the lower paved parking area, walk across the suspension bridge over the Snoqualmie River and away from the river up toward a wood picnic shelter. To the

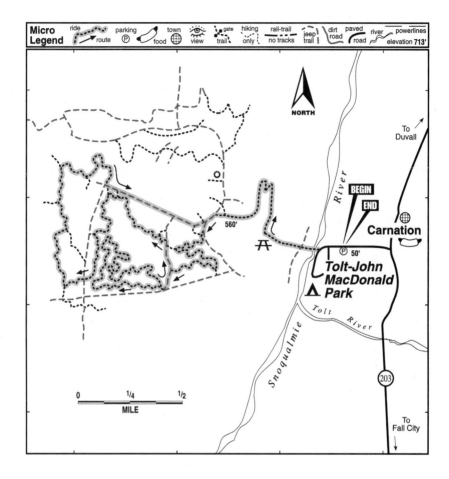

Micro Legend

ride route · parking ℗ · town food ⊕ · view 👁 · gate trail, hiking only — rail-trail no tracks · jeep trail · dirt road · paved road · river · powerlines · elevation 713'

right of the shelter, find a singletrack and start climbing. It's a tough climb, and small chain rings are a good thing. The trail traverses up the steep bank. There's a short drop followed by a short walk around a large stump, then a series of baby switchbacks. **Woof!** At **0.7 mile**, the trail finally levels out. Ignore two trails on the right at **0.8 mile**. At **0.9 mile**, reach a 5-way intersection (**Whoa**—remember this location!) of two trails and three jeep roads. Turn left on a jeep road, then almost immediately turn right onto a singletrack. When the trail divides at **1.0 mile**, bear left onto Mystery Trail.

From here the way is winding and twisty, with sharp ups and downs and extra tight turns. Beware the mud holes and slick roots that add to the riding challenge much of the year. At **1.3 miles**, reach a fork and bear left, now rolling on Oxbow Trail. **Whoa**—when the trail divides at **1.6 miles**, take a hard right turn that's easy to ride right by. At **1.9 miles**, arrive at a T and turn left on the wider, faster Cross

Big smiles at the top of the hillclimb

Quadrant Trail. Don't go too fast because at **2.0 miles**, just before reaching a road, you need to find two trails that begin from the same point on the right. Facing the two trails, take the one on the left, Double Bypass Trail, and start the twisties again. Reach a fork at **2.2 miles** and go right. At **2.4 miles**, arrive at a 4-way and take a hard right.

The fun, technical, user-built trail continues, and at some point over the next long stretch Double Bypass becomes The Burn. Next comes an unbelievable series of eleven straight left-hand turns. Start counting. When the trail splits at **3.6 miles**—reach a fork and bear left. Bear left again at **3.7 miles**. At **3.8 miles**, you've made a loop—turn left and then immediately left again. You should be riding away from the road on Cross Quadrant. Stay left at **4.0 miles** and again at **4.1 miles**. Immediately reach a T and—guess what—turn left! You're on Cousins Trail now and back in the tight twisties again. At **4.5 miles**, reach a fork and bear left. When the trail divides at **4.8 miles**, go left again. Reach a T at **4.9 miles**, and turn left on MLR Trail. At **5.2 miles**, arrive at a fork and bear left, now pedaling along Bypass Trail.

Reach a T at **5.5 miles** and, remarkably, the streak of left turns ends—take a right and cross the dirt road. Find the singletrack on the opposite side of the road and take it. Now you're on Blair Witch Trail. When the trail divides at **5.7 miles**, go left, descending quickly. Reach a fork at **5.9 miles** and bear left, climbing now. Ignore a trail on the left at **6.1 miles**. At **6.3 miles**, reach a fork and turn left on Toothpick Trail. At **6.7 miles**, reach a 5-way intersection of three roads and two trails—turn left onto the dirt road. From here, stay on the road until the major 5-way intersection at the top of the hillclimb, ignoring one trail on the right and then three trail crossings at **6.8 miles**, **6.9 miles**, and **7.2 miles**. At **7.25 miles**, reach the 5-way (mentioned at the 0.9-mile point) at the top of the hillclimb. From here, bear slightly left to gain the trail that drops down to the Snoqualmie River, the bridge, and the parking area at **8.1 miles**.

NOTES:

_____

_____

Ride 34 ✳ ✳ ✳

TAPEWORM

Distance	**3.8 miles**, lollipop loop
Terrain	Technical singletrack; micro climbs, **minimal elevation gain**
Duration	1 to 2 hours
Travel	18 miles from Seattle
Skill Level	Expert
Season	Year round
Map	USGS: *Renton*
Explorability	Moderate

Prelude

From a briar-patch beginning, the myth of the Tapeworm Trail has grown large in Seattle mountain bike mythology, and for good reason. Where else can you test your skills on trails named Tapeworm, Mr. DNA, or Crop Circles? Or pedal near the famed Ewok Village, now gone like the lost city of Atlantis? Not often enough. With slow, super-narrow hairpin turns and switchbacks every five feet, you'll soon know what it's like to be a worm in a sick gut. But don't cut the switchbacks or else the magic of the continuous, one-way trail will be ruined, and the patient might die.

Driving Directions

Take Interstate 405 south to Exit 4 in Renton. Off the ramp, merge with Sunset Blvd. N. Turn right on Bronson Way N., cross the bridge, then turn left on Mill Avenue S. Go straight through the light, and turn left on Renton Avenue S. After a steep hill, turn left on S. 7th Street, then veer right on Beacon Way S. to Phillip Arnold Park. Stop at the parking lot adjacent to the baseball diamond.

The Ride

From the paved parking area adjacent to the playfields, ride up Beacon Way through a gate that is usually closed. At the top of the hill, **0.25 mile**, meet the first of many sets of power lines. Turn to the right, pass through several concrete barriers, and ride along a narrow dirt road. At **0.3 mile**, turn back to the left on a narrow trail. The trail rounds the corner of a substation. Then at **0.4 mile**, turn right on a lesser trail into the brush: the beginning of Mr. DNA. After numerous twists and turns, ups and downs, finish the double helix at a T—turn right, **0.8 mile**. You have seen your tapeworm future.

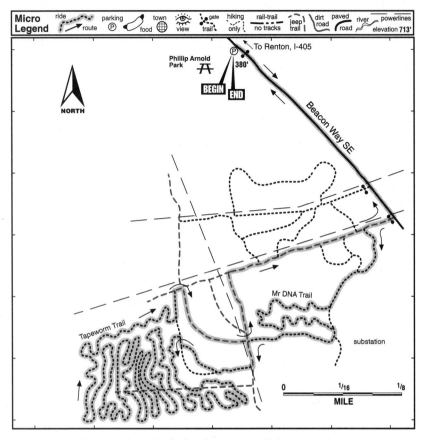

At **0.85 mile**, take the right fork. The singletrack drops to a 4-way intersection at **0.95 mile**; go left onto a dirt road. Immediately a singletrack exits to the right—take that trail. The trail drops, bearing to the right. When the trail forks at **1.0 mile**, bear right. At **1.05 miles**, find a faint trail on the left and take it. This is the start of the Worm. Once you enter, bailing out and bushwhacking home is unacceptable. Right from the start, the trail snakes frantically, coiling and recoiling. After fourteen charmed switchbacks, the trail ends at a T at **3.15 miles**—turn left. Ride to a 4-way intersection and turn right, then immediately turn right again onto a singletrack. At **3.3 miles**, reach another 4-way intersection and turn left. Bear right at the immediate fork and ride straight to a T at **3.35 miles**. Turn right and ride up this dirt road, adjacent to a big set of power lines, to a T at Beacon Way S. at **3.55 miles**. Turn left and pedal back to Phillip Arnold Park, **3.8 miles**.

NOTES:

Ride 35 ⊗ ⊗

LAKE YOUNGS

Distance	**9.9 miles**, loop
Terrain	Dirt trails, dirt roads; gentle hills, one short steep hill, **cumulative gain: 600 ft.**
Duration	1 to 2 hours
Travel	19 miles from Seattle
Skill Level	Beginner
Season	Year round
Map	USGS: *Renton*
Explorability	Low
Restrictions	Day-use only
More Info	King County Parks, 206-296-4232, www.metrokc.gov/parks/

Prelude

Lake Youngs is part of the Seattle water system, so the lake is surrounded by a tall fence, and security is tight. Though the lake is never actually visible, ignore that frustration and enjoy this easy, wooded loop. Deer are common inside the fence. Though it's an easy, beginner trail for the most part, a few sections are rough.

Driving Directions

From Bellevue, go south on Interstate 405 to Exit 4. After the exit ramp merges with Sunset Blvd., proceed several blocks, then turn left onto Highway 169, the Maple Valley Road. Zero out your odometer here. At 2.2 miles, turn right onto 140th Way S.E. At 4.0 miles, turn left on S.E. Petrovitsky Road. At 5.4 miles, turn right onto Old Petrovitsky Road. At 5.9 miles, find the Lake Youngs Trail parking area on the right.

Crossing Seattle's water pipe near Lake Youngs

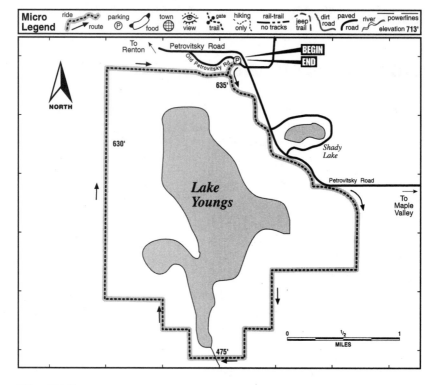

ride route parking ⓟ town food view gate hiking trail only rail-trail no tracks jeep trail dirt road paved road river powerlines elevation 713'

The Ride

Begin from the gravel parking area at the King County park next to Lake Youngs. Find the trail that leaves from the parking area. This trail accesses the loop around Lake Youngs. At **0.15 mile** from the parking area, reach the Lake Youngs loop trail and turn left. The wide trail follows the fence that encloses the reservoir. At **2.3 miles**, reach the intersection of 184th Avenue S.E. and S.E. Lake Youngs Road. Cross over the water pipe and continue following the wide gravel trail alongside the fence. At **6.5 miles**, reach the corner of 148th Avenue S.E. and S.E. 216th Street. Take a right, still following the fence but now paralleling 148th S.E. and winding clockwise around the lake (wherever it is). At **9.6 miles**, begin climbing a short, steep hill. You may have to walk it. At **9.75 miles**, you've completed the loop. Take a left onto the trail that returns to the parking area, **9.9 miles**.

NOTES:

_____

_____

Ride 36 ⊗

LAKE WILDERNESS

Distance	**4.0 miles**, out and back
Terrain	Gravel rail-trail; flat, one very short hill, **minimal elevation gain**
Duration	1 hour
Travel	26 miles from Seattle
Skill Level	Beginner
Season	Year round
Maps	USGS: *Auburn, Renton*
Explorability	Low
Restrictions	Day-use only
More Info	King County Parks, 206-296-4298, www.metrokc.gov/parks/

Prelude

This flat ride traverses an old railroad grade above Lake Wilderness. There's one very short hill to walk up, and the gravel tread might be loose in spots, but other than that it's easy. The grade, through a light forest and past some homes, affords views of the lake below. It's perfect for the first-time mountain bicyclist or, given the park facilities at Lake Wilderness Park, the whole family. Note: The trail is managed by King County, but the beach and picnic area are now run by the city of Maple Valley.

Driving Directions

From Bellevue, go south on Interstate 405 to Exit 4. After the exit ramp merges with Sunset Blvd., proceed several blocks, then turn left onto Highway 169, the Maple Valley Road. Zero out your odometer here. At 11.5 miles, turn right onto Witte Road S.E. At 12.3 miles, turn left on S.E. 248th Street. At 12.5 miles, reach a 4-way: Go straightish, continuing on S.E. 248th Street, toward Lake Wilderness Center. At 12.7 miles, park behind the building.

Lake Wilderness

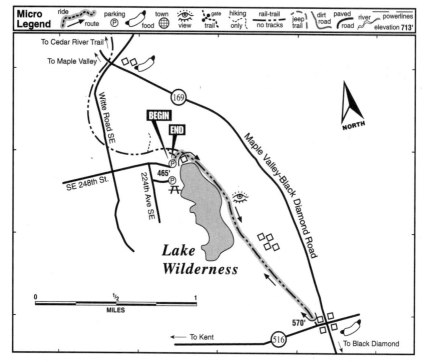

The Ride

Beginning from behind the center building at Lake Wilderness Park, take the wide dirt trail that begins at the far end of the parking area. At **0.1 mile**, reach a fork and bear right. Walk up a short but steep hill. At **0.2 mile**, reach a T at the rail-trail. Turn right (south), riding to a gate. Pedal around the gate and continue along the wide gravel trail. The trail traverses the east side of Lake Wilderness. Stay on the main trail. Reach Highway 516, the Kent-Kangley Road, at **2.0 miles**. Turn around here and ride back to the parking area for a total of **4.0 miles**.

Addition

If you still want more when you get back to the gate just above the parking area, continue north on the rail-trail. It winds 1.8 miles to a junction with the Cedar River Trail. This out-and-back jaunt adds 3.6 miles onto the ride.

NOTES:

_____

_____

_____

_____

Ride 37 ✵✵✵

THE WOODS

Distance	**5.3 miles**, lollipop loop
Terrain	Twisty singletrack, dirt road; micro climbs, **minimal elevation gain**
Duration	1 to 2 hours
Travel	33 miles from Seattle
Skill Level	Advanced
Season	Spring, summer, fall
Map	USGS: *Auburn*
Explorability	Extreme
Restrictions	Private property

Prelude

If you like the skill-building trails at Tolt-MacDonald (see Ride 33), the Worm (see Ride 34), or at Paradise Valley (see Ride 23), you'll love the Woods along Highway 169 near Four Corners. It's all twisty, unmarked, user-built singletrack with few climbs longer than ten feet, where foot dabs and getting your bars stuck between trees are the primary concern. This 5-mile loop is just an introduction to the area and represents only a small portion of the trails. But the Woods will likely be developed soon, and in fact some trails out there have already been bulldozed to make room for card-house mansions, so ride it while you can.

Driving Directions

Take Interstate 405 south to Exit 4 in Renton. Zero out your odometer as you spill off the interstate onto Sunset Blvd. N. At 0.4 mile, turn left onto Highway 169, following the signs for Maple Valley. Cross Highway 516 at 14.5 miles. At 16.9 miles, just before entering Black Diamond, find a small paved pullout on the right.

At one with the Woods

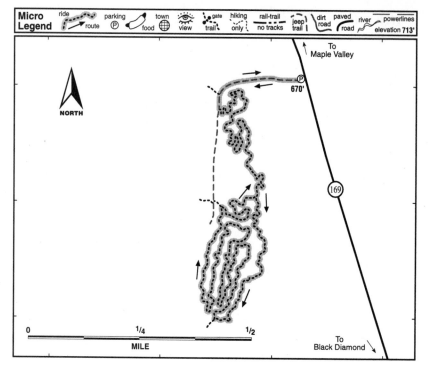

The Ride

From the edge of Hwy 169, ride around the gate and down the doubletrack, descending slightly. The doubletrack runs straight for about one quarter-mile, then bends to the left. Bypass a singletrack on the right. At **0.3 mile**, find a singletrack on the left and take it. From here, advanced skills and a firm grip are required as the trails twists relentlessly through second-growth forest. Carouseling around huge stumps, barreling through the gaps between trees, edging along tricky sidecuts, climbing 10 feet, then slaloming down—the trail is non-stop, and it's all fun.

When you reach a fork at **1.2 miles**, bear left. The trail continues winding and twisting. At **1.7 miles**, the trail divides—take the right fork. At **3.5 miles**, reach a fork and bear right. (The left prong crosses the doubletrack to a rat's nest of user-built singletrack, a place where trying to know where you are misses the point.) At **4.1 miles**, you've closed the lollipop and returned to the fork at 1.2 miles—take the left fork. The trail pops out at the doubletrack at **5.0 miles**. Turn right and ride up the doubletrack to Hwy 169, **5.3 miles**.

NOTES:

Ride 38 ✸✸✸

BLACK DIAMOND LAKE

Distance	**8.9 miles**, loop
Terrain	Wide dirt trails, paved roads; rolling, **minimal elevation gain**
Duration	2 to 3 hours
Travel	35 miles from Seattle
Skill Level	Advanced
Season	Year round
Map	USGS: *Auburn*
Explorability	High
Restrictions	Private property

Prelude

With each edition of *Kissing the Trail*, a new incarnation of this ride is born. The land is a hodgepodge of private property, and changes come fast and furious, so a trail today could be a clearcut or housing development tomorrow. This version completely ignores the land north of the Auburn-Black Diamond Road and focuses on old and new trails to the south. Wide to narrow, zippy to slow, the trails and jeep tracks are all ragged or ad hoc in some way. Overgrown blackberries are such a problem in one section, it's really a miracle I still have arms attached. Of course, that's no issue for serious mountain bikers out searching for a good adventure. Exploration is fun, and that's the point here.

All bundled up on the way to Black Diamond Lake

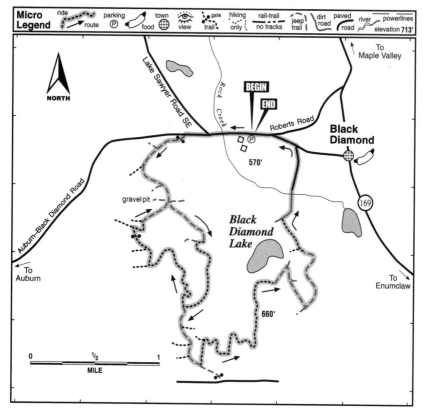

Driving Directions

Take Interstate 405 south to Exit 4 in Renton. Zero out your odometer as you spill off the interstate onto Sunset Blvd. N. At 0.4 mile, turn left onto Highway 169, following the signs for Maple Valley. Cross Hwy 516 at 14.5 miles. At 17.8 miles, just before Black Diamond's main street, turn right onto Roberts Road. At 18.6 miles, find the King County Library on the left. Park in the library's lot.

The Ride

Beginning from the King County Library parking lot, turn left onto Roberts Road (Auburn-Black Diamond Road). Pedal west, away from Black Diamond. When the road splits at **0.5 mile**, bear left. **Whoa**—at **0.6 mile**, turn left, and ride over a berm onto a wide dirt road. The road forks at **0.8 mile**—bear left on the main route. Stay to the left again at **0.9 mile**. At **1.0 mile**, ride alongside a gravel pit. Keep the pit on your right, ignoring trails into it. **Whoa**—at the 5-way intersection at **1.1 mile**, take the easy, shallow left (not the hard left). The way becomes a jeep trail bending first to the left and then to the right and climbing a short hill. Reach a fork at **1.6 miles**, and turn left.

The wide trail is rocky, but also zippy and fast. Reach a fork at **2.3 miles** and turn right. When the trail divides at **2.8 miles**, go right. At **3.0 miles**, ignore the lesser trail on the left. Pass around an old gate, then reach a fork, **3.3 miles**, and turn right. Turn right again at **3.4 miles**. Ignore a trail back on the left at **3.5 miles**. Cross over a berm, then ride past the gravel pit again—keep it on your left. You've completed a loop when you reach a fork at **3.7 miles** (same fork as 1.1 miles)—turn right and climb the short hill one more time.

Ignore a trail on the right at **4.2 miles**. When the way forks again at **4.9 miles**, go left (last time around you turned right at this junction). Ignore one lesser trail on the left then two on the right. **Whoa**—at **5.5 miles**, take the faint trail on the left (if you

Fall singletrack near Black Diamond Lake

reach a gate at a paved road, you've gone too far). Reach a fork at **5.6 miles** and head down the narrow right prong. Ignore a faint trail on the right, then pass by a house and along a fence line at **6.0 miles**. From here, it's up and down on twisty, brushy (okay, overgrown) singletrack.

The trail ends at a beat-up dirt road, **6.5 miles**. Ride down the rough road to a fork, **6.7 miles**, and turn right. Quickly arrive at another fork and bear right. Reach a T at **7.1 miles**—this time turn left. At **7.4 miles**, the road narrows to a wide trail. Ignore a faint trail on the left at **7.6 miles**. From here, the trail drops precipitously.

At **7.9 miles**, the trail ends at a dirt road. Turn right, ride a short distance and veer left, away from the gate. The road, Abrams Avenue, soon becomes paved. Reach a T at **8.5 miles**, and turn left onto Morgan Street. At **8.8 miles**, Morgan Street ends at Roberts Road. Turn left and ride a few hundred yards to the King County Library on the left, **8.9 miles**, to complete the loop.

NOTES:

_____

_____

_____

_____

Destination 39 ✺✺✺

KANASKAT-PALMER STATE PARK

Distance	**2 to 3 miles**, loops
Terrain	Narrow and wide dirt trails; healthy climbing from entrance to river
Duration	1 to 2 hours
Travel	36 miles from Seattle
Skill level	Intermediate
Season	Spring, summer, fall (sensitive trails: avoid during wet weather)
Map	*Kanaskat-Palmer State Park* map
Explorability	Moderate
Restrictions	State Parks vehicle fee, dogs on leash
More Info	Washington State Parks, 360-902-8844, www.parks.wa.gov

Prelude

Located along a surging length of the Green River, the 320-acre Kanaskat-Palmer State Park is heavily used by boaters in search of challenging rapids. The river makes it a scenic location for the campground, the day-use picnic area, and the trails. Wide and narrow trails wend their way throughout the park from the boundary near Cumberland-Kanaskat Road down to the river and from the campground to the day-use area. Though distances are limited, it's a fun place to play on your bike with your family. The park's three miles of trails can be extended by repeating loops. Get the park map and explore. The park gets lots of use, so be considerate to others on the trails. Note: There are preliminary plans to build a trail linking this park with Flaming Geyser State Park, and that would be very cool. Stay tuned.

Driving Directions

From Bellevue, take Interstate 405 south to Exit 4. Zero out your odometer as you merge with Sunset Blvd. N. At 0.4 mile, turn left on Highway 169. At 14.5 miles, turn left on Highway 516, the Kent-Kangley Road. At 18 miles, bear right on Retreat-Kanaskat Road. At 21.2 miles, turn right on Cumberland-Kanaskat Road. At 23 miles, find Kanaskat-Palmer State Park on the right.

NOTES:

_____

_____

Ride 40 ⊕

NOLTE STATE PARK

Distance	**1.6 miles**, loop
Terrain	Wide dirt trail; **minimal elevation gain**
Duration	Less than 1 hour
Travel	40 miles from Seattle
Skill Level	Beginner
Season	Spring, summer, fall (sensitive trail: avoid during wet weather)
Map	USGS: *Cumberland*
Explorability	Low
Restrictions	State Parks vehicle fee, day-use only, dogs on leash
More Info	Washington State Parks, 360-902-8844, www.parks.wa.gov

Prelude

Perhaps the easiest ride in the book, this short loop around Deep Lake is designed for families with children—definitely not for anyone who wants fast riding or lots of miles. The ride is easy and the surrounding forests beautiful. The swimming beach and picnic area make it a versatile spot for the entire brood.

Reflecting on Deep Lake

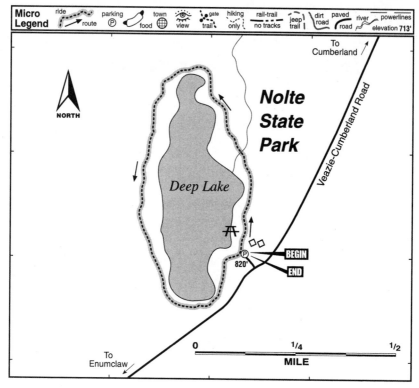

Driving Directions

From Bellevue, take Interstate 405 south to Exit 4. Zero out your odometer as you merge with Sunset Blvd. N. At 0.4 mile, turn left onto Highway 169, toward Maple Valley. At 14.5 miles, turn left on Highway 516, the Kent-Kangley Road. At 18 miles, bear right on Retreat-Kanaskat Road. At 21.2 miles, turn right on Cumberland-Kanaskat Road. Through Cumberland, 25.3 miles, the road becomes the Veazie-Cumberland Road. At 26.8 miles, find Nolte State Park on the right.

The Ride

From the parking lot, ride about 100 yards to the kiosk near the picnic area and the beach. Between the picnic tables and the ranger's residence, find the paved trail that heads off to the right. After a few pedal strokes, the pavement ends. From here the wide hardpack trail rolls easily. The tour around the lake ends back at the picnic area, **1.5 miles**. Complete the loop by pedaling back to the parking area, **1.6 miles**.

NOTES:

Ride 41 ✿✿✿

DASH POINT STATE PARK

Distance	**4.1 miles**, loop
Terrain	Dirt trails, paved road; steep hills, **cumulative gain: 450 ft.**
Duration	1 hour
Travel	25 miles from Seattle
Skill Level	Intermediate
Season	Summer, fall (sensitive trail: avoid during wet weather)
Map	*Dash Point State Park* map
Explorability	Moderate
Restrictions	State Parks vehicle fee, dogs on leash
More Info	Washington State Parks, 360-902-8844, www.parks.wa.gov

Prelude

Dash Point State Park is a busy campground during the summer, especially on weekends, so the riding is probably best during the week. The narrow dirt trails through the woods near the campground provide fun, occasionally technical, riding. Because of several steep slopes, stairs have been built to improve the trail. These must be walked. Be extremely courteous to all other trail users. The ranger has said that mountain bicycles are allowed "for the time being," meaning as long as there aren't too many complaints.

Puget Sound from the beach at Dash Point

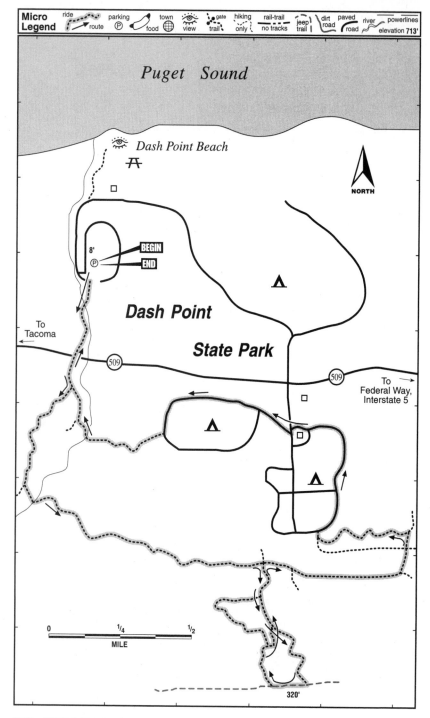

Micro Legend

ride → route · parking ℗ · town / food ⊕ · view · gate / hiking trail only · rail-trail / no tracks · jeep trail · dirt road · paved road · river / powerlines · elevation 713'

Puget Sound

👁 *Dash Point Beach*

⛺

NORTH

8'
℗ BEGIN
END

Dash Point

To Tacoma

509

State Park

509

To Federal Way, Interstate 5

⛺

⛺

⛺

0   ¹/₄   ¹/₂
MILE

320'

Driving Directions

From Seattle, drive south on Interstate 5. Take Federal Way Exit 143. Zero out your odometer at the end of the exit and bear right, traveling west on S. 320th Street. At 4.6 miles, 320th Street ends at a T. Turn right onto 47th Avenue S.W. At 5.0 miles, turn left onto S.W. Dash Point Road. At 5.9 miles, find Dash Point State Park on the right. Drive all the way down to the day-use parking lot near the beach.

The Ride

From the parking lot, ride away from the beach. Find the trail that travels under the Highway 509 bridge far above. Pedal up the wide trail to **0.3 mile** where you'll find a trail up the bank to the right. The walking begins. Push your bike about 250 yards up the trail before you can ride again. At **0.4 mile**, cross a creek and continue up. The trail elbows left upon reaching the top of the hill at **0.5 mile**. At **0.8 mile**, walk across a bridge.

Reach a 4-way intersection at **1.0 mile**. Turn up the hill to the right. The trail forks twice over the next quarter-mile: each time take the left trail. When the trail divides again at **1.4 miles**, turn right onto a wider jeep trail. Turn right, back onto a singletrack, at **1.5 miles**. At **1.7 miles**, continue on the main trail—straight. At **1.75 miles**, take the left fork. This trail returns you to the earlier 4-way intersection. You've now clocked **2.0 miles**. Turn right at the 4-way intersection.

At **2.15** and **2.5 miles**, take the left fork each time. Just past the second fork, reach a 4-way intersection: Go straight. At **2.65 miles**, take the sharp left fork. At **3.0 miles**, meet a wide trail and turn right. A few pedal strokes farther, reach Campsite 58. Turn right onto the paved road. At **3.1 miles**, stay to the right, then at **3.3 miles** reach the park entrance.

From the pay station at the park entrance, turn right. Ride around the campsite loop counterclockwise, to Campsite 15. Find the sign toward the beach. Turn right onto the trail toward the beach, **3.6 miles**. Walk down the wooden steps at **3.7 miles**. Then ride down the main trail—ignoring spurs—back to the parking lot and the beach, **4.1 miles**.

NOTES:

_____

_____

_____

_____

Ride 42 ✹✹✹

VICTOR FALLS

Distance	**7.8 miles**, lollipop loop
Terrain	Dirt trails, dirt roads; rolling hills, some steep (but no long) climbs, **cumulative gain: 750 ft.**
Duration	1 to 3 hours
Travel	43 miles from Seattle
Skill Level	Intermediate plus
Season	Year round
Maps	USGS: *Sumner, Orting*
Explorability	Extreme
Restrictions	Closed mid-November to mid-January, private property

Prelude

The huge parcel of land south of Highway 410, bounded by the Puyallup River to the west, the Carbon River to the south, and 198th Avenue E. to the east, commonly known as Victor Falls, is one of the premier mountain bike spots in the south Puget Sound region, and it's all private property. A phenomenal number of trails and dirt roads, ranging from easy to technical, crisscross the site, making for excellent exploring. If you want to get lost, this is the place to ride. This loop functions as an excellent introduction to Victor Falls. If you can find it, check out Jim Hendricks' map of the area, which remains remarkably accurate despite logging and some blocks of new houses. Of course more new houses are slated for this area,

Hillside Farms Christmas Trees—where it all begins

and logging (in advance of development) may obliterate or re-route even more trails. So be prepared for changes. It must be noted that for years our heroes at Hillside Farms Christmas Trees have allowed mountain bikers to park in the lot from January through the end of October. Don't trash the parking area! Please respect the closure dates so they can sell trees—and they'd sure like it if you bought your Christmas tree there. It should also be noted that the landowner tolerates non-motorized use; be a good citizen out on the trails so we can keep it that way.

Driving Directions

From Bellevue, take Interstate 405 south to Exit 2 in Tukwila. Then head south on Highway 167 toward Puyallup. Take the Highway 410 Exit toward Yakima, and drive east just over 5.5 miles to Bonney Lake. Turn right on South Prairie Road E., and set your odometer to zero. At 1.5 miles, turn right on 214th Avenue E. At 2.4 miles, turn right on 120th Street E. Reach a T at 3.2 miles, and turn left onto 198th Avenue E. At 3.7 miles, find Hillside Farms Christmas Trees on the right. Show some mountain bike courtesy: Don't litter or relieve yourself in the parking lot.

The Ride

From the parking area, pedal away from 198th Avenue, up a dirt road known as the Main Access Road. At **0.2 miles**, pass around a gate. Almost immediately, reach a 4-way and turn left onto a wide trail known as Elevator. Right away it narrows and ascends steeply. Stay on the main trail as you climb, ignoring two trails on the right. The trail crests and seems to end at a dirt road, **0.8 mile**. Across the road on the right, though, the trail continues. From here, the trail, known as Route 66, winds then drops. Pass straight through a 4-way at **1.0 mile**. At **1.2 miles**, reach a T and turn left. At **1.4 miles**, reach another T and turn right. Descend and then wind around a swale of low brush that contains the hulk of a white truck. Arrive at a T at **1.8 miles**, and turn left. The trail ends at 198th Avenue at **1.9 miles**—turn right and ride alongside the paved road.

At **2.1 miles**, find a singletrack that exits the road on the right and take it. The trail winds and twists. Ride straight through a 4-way at **2.4 miles**. When the trail divides, **2.7 miles**, stay to the right. Pedal straight through another 4-way at **2.9 miles**. Reach a gravel road at **3.2 miles**—hop on the slightly technical singletrack that continues on the opposite side. When the trail forks, bear right. Reach a T at a narrow road, **3.3 miles**, and go right, descending. At **3.6 miles**, reach a T and turn right. The narrow road forks at **3.7 miles**—bear left. At **3.8 miles**, immediately before reaching a T, turn right on a singletrack. **Whoa**—this is an easy turn to miss.

The trail, narrow and winding, heads north and is at times brushy and overgrown, as blackberry vines lunge at unprotected skin and spiders, web and all, catch rides on the first bike through. After some good pedaling unmolested by a dividing trail, you'll reach a wide dirt road, **4.3 miles**. The singletrack begins again on the opposite side of the road after a short jog to the right. At **4.4 miles**, ride straight through a 4-way. Stay on the main trail, known as Mustang, as it sweeps back and forth, in and out of the trees, then finally out again. Ignore a trail back on the right at **5.5 miles**. Just beyond, the trail splits again and this time bear right.

From here, still out in the open of a clearcut, the singletrack gradually widens. Reach a 4-way of dirt roads at **5.7 miles** and proceed straight ahead. At **5.9 miles**,

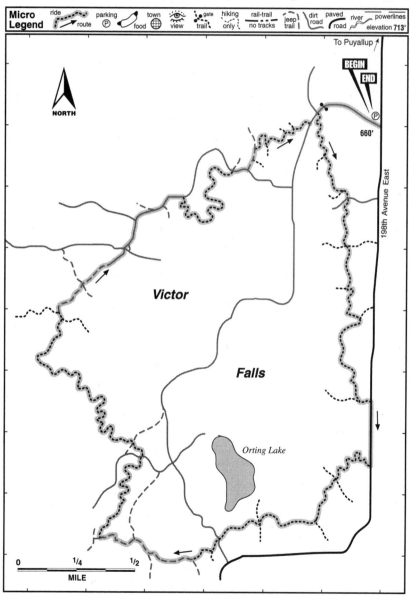

The Cut Your Bars Trail at Victor Falls

arrive at a complicated 4-way intersection at a major gravel road—turn right onto the wide gravel road, ignoring the lesser cut-off road immediately prior on your right. Ride toward a conspicuous stand of trees about one quarter-mile ahead. When the road forks at **6.0 miles**, bear right. Ignore a lesser road on the left at **6.1 miles**. Bear left at the fork at **6.2 miles**. Just when you've had enough of the road riding, find a singletrack on the right, **6.4 miles**, that enters that conspicuous stand of trees. This trail is called Cut Your Bars, although after years of use it's not quite that technical anymore.

At **6.7 miles**, the trail pops out at a 4-way (three roads, plus your trail). Turn right on the road. When the road forks at **6.9 miles**, go left on a narrow dirt road. Ignore a tasty looking singletrack on the right at **7.0 miles**. But at **7.1 miles**, find another singletrack and turn right. This small area, often referred to as Snickers, bound by the narrow road behind and the Access Road ahead, contains a maze of fun, zippy trails—and a few tours through the maze are well worth your while. At **7.2 miles**, reach a fork and bear left. At **7.3 miles**, reach a fork and go right. Bear right again at the next fork, then drop down to reach Access Road at **7.5 miles**, then turn left. When you arrive at the 4-way, **7.6 miles**, you've connected the loop. Go straight through the 4-way, around the gate, and glide back to the parking area at the Christmas tree farm, **7.8 miles**.

NOTES:

_____

_____

Ride 43 ✪ ✪ ✪

MUD MOUNTAIN

Distance	**4.2 miles**, out and back
Terrain	Singletrack, dirt roads; short, stout climbs, **cumulative gain: 350 ft.**
Duration	1 to 2 hours
Travel	45 miles from Seattle
Skill Level	Intermediate
Season	Year round
Map	Green Trails: *Enumclaw*
Explorability	Low
Restrictions	Day-use only
More Info	U.S. Army Corps of Engineers, 206-764-3717, www.nws.usace.army.mil/opdiv/mmd/index.htm

Prelude

I call the Mud Mountain Rim Trail transitional singletrack. This short stretch of trail requires only intermediate skill level, and it's short. Once you're comfortable here (and after lots of solid workouts), you'll be ready to graduate to Ranger Creek (see Ride 48), Suntop (see Ride 45), and the other more challenging rides out Highway 410. With a great picnic area and playground, Mud Mountain Dam Recreation Site—maintained by the U.S. Army Corps of Engineers—is also a great place for families. The kids get slides and swings; Mom and Dad get singletrack.

Driving Directions

From Seattle, head east on Interstate 90, south on Interstate 405 to Exit 4, then south on State Highway 169 to Enumclaw. In Enumclaw, take State Hwy 410 south toward Mount Rainier. As you leave town, pass milepost 26 and set your odometer to zero. At 3.9 miles, turn right on Mud Mountain Dam Road. At 6.4 miles, reach Mud Mountain Dam Recreation Site.

The Ride

From the parking area, ride back to the entrance gate and turn right on the trail that parallels the fence. After 50 yards, the trail bends left, away from the fence. At **0.3 mile**, the trail ends at a dirt road—turn right and ride down the road. At **0.5 mile**, take the trail on the left, which bends around a large cedar. Reach another road at **0.8 mile** and turn right. Almost immediately you'll find the Rim Trail on the left.

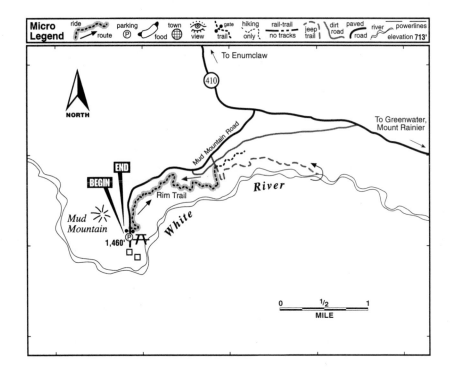

Micro Legend: ride route · parking Ⓟ · town food ⊕ · view · gate trail · hiking only · rail-trail no tracks · jeep trail · dirt road · paved road · river · powerlines · elevation 713'

To Enumclaw

410

NORTH

Mud Mountain Road

To Greenwater, Mount Rainier

END

BEGIN

Rim Trail

River

Mud Mountain

White

1,460'

Ⓟ

0   ½   1
MILE

From here, the trail descends for a short pitch then noodles across a series of narrow wood planks that protect a boggy lowland. At **1.2 miles**, the trail crosses a dirt road, bears to the left, and passes a small bathroom. After a few more turns, you will emerge from the dark forest and ride along a wooden fence that borders the cliffs that overlook the White River gorge. Pass a picnic table here, **1.4 miles**. Just beyond the viewpoint, the trail bends away from the rim's edge and climbs for a short distance, possibly requiring a push. At **2.1 miles**, reach a 4-way intersection.

From this 4-way intersection, several options present themselves. A left turn leads immediately into Weyerhauser's White River Tree Farm. Dirt roads and trails are everywhere. An interesting, though less maintained, trail crosses the road and continues along the river valley's rim. You can also turn right and glide down the dirt road to the banks of the White River. Or you can turn around here and ride back to the parking area, **4.2 miles**.

NOTES:

_____

_____

SKOOKUM FLATS

Distance	**11.5 miles**, loop
Terrain	Technical singletrack, dirt roads; short, steep hills, some walking, **cumulative gain: 1,600 ft.**
Duration	2 to 4 hours
Travel	66 miles from Seattle
Skill Level	Advanced
Season	Summer, early fall (sensitive trail: avoid during wet weather)
Map	Green Trails: *Greenwater*
Explorability	Low
Restrictions	NW Forest Pass
More Info	Mount Baker-Snoqualmie National Forest, Snoqualmie District (Enumclaw), 360-825-6585, www.fs.fed.us/r6/mbs/

Prelude

This has been called Washington's best ride, but that writer clearly hadn't ridden enough Northwest trails. While Skookum Flats Trail is worthy of some mention, perhaps even honorable (it's a great trail and well-known), I wouldn't bestow the "best" moniker on it, especially with so many epic (and less used) trails nearby. However, for those interested in fun, technical singletrack through old-growth forest along the rugged White River, Skookum Flats is the ticket. And though the cumulative elevation gain is hearty, there's no long dirt road climb.

High water on the Skookum Flats Trail

Driving Directions

From Seattle, head east on Interstate 90, south on Interstate 405 to Exit 4, then south on Highway 169 to Enumclaw. In Enumclaw, take Highway 410 south toward Mount Rainier. As you leave town, pass milepost 26 and set your odometer to zero. At 28.4 miles, just past milepost 54, turn right on Buck Creek Road. Cross over the White River, and take the first left into the parking area.

The Ride

Find the Skookum Flats Trail 1194 across the dirt road from the parking area. When the trail splits at **0.1 mile**, take the left fork. At **0.3 mile**, take the right fork. After a hairpin turn, cross a short bridge. The trail traverses a precipitous slope and has many roots and tight turns. Ride across another wooden bridge at **1.1 miles**. At **1.3 miles**, reach a rocky ascent. At **1.4 miles**, reach a fork and bear left (a suspension bridge over the river and a trail up to Hwy 410 exits right). The next one quarter-mile ascends via steps, roots, short bridges, and large rocks. The trail levels out at **1.6 miles**. At **1.8 miles**, take the right fork and traverse the bank well above the White River. The next several miles are technical and difficult, a hike-a-bike for some. Ride through stands of old growth, with limited but lovely views of the White River.

After the **4.5-mile** point, the trail becomes less difficult, and at **4.8 miles** it reaches a clearing. Take the right fork here,

One of Skookum's few straightaways

continuing on singletrack. From here, stay on the main trail, paralleling the river. At **5.8 miles**, reach Forest Road 73. Turn right and quickly cross a paved bridge over the White River. After the bridge, **5.9 miles**, find Trail 1204A on the right and take it. After three short bridges, this trail delivers you to Dalles Campground. At **6.4 miles**, just before entering the campground, you'll find a 700-year-old Douglas fir that is nearly 10 feet in diameter.

From the huge tree, ride across the narrow bridge and through the campground, staying to the left. Arrive at the entrance of the campground at **6.9 miles**. Cross Hwy 410 and ride up FR 7150. At **7.1 miles**, the road levels and bends to the right, then

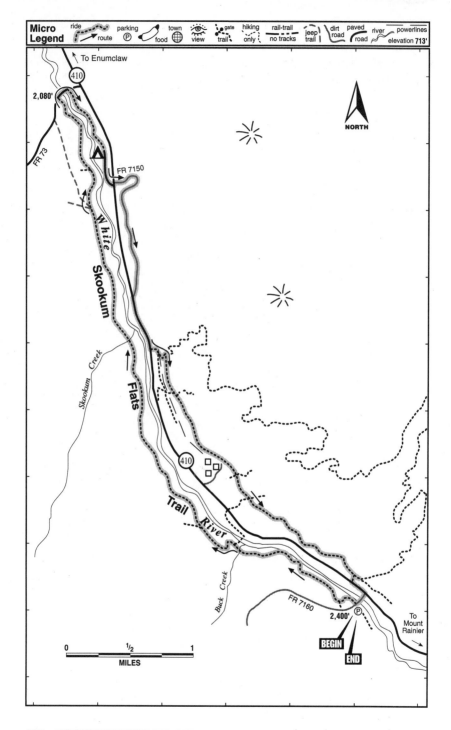

bends left and parallels the highway. Ignore a road on the left at **7.4 miles**. Stay on the main road as there are many driveways to cabins along this way. At **8.0 miles**, reach Highway 410 again. Turn left onto it. At **8.6 miles**, find a small pullout on the left side of the road, and a trail. White River Trail 1199 climbs up a short bank away from Highway 410, first bending to the right, then to the left after a steep climb. The ascent ends at the **8.9-mile** point, where you'll find a trail junction: Bear left to remain on the White River Trail. Reach another intersection at **9.2 miles**—again continue straight on Trail 1199.

A Douglas fir along the White River

At **9.65 miles**, enter a clearing that denotes the edge of Camp Sheppard. The trail becomes a jeep trail here. But at **9.75 miles**, with some buildings on the right, find a trail and a sign marked Trail on the left. **Whoa**—this is easy to miss. Take the trail on the left and then bear right, riding above the buildings at Camp Sheppard. After this turn, stay on the main trail. At **10.0 miles**, arrive at another intersection—continue straight on Trail 1199. At **10.3 miles**, reach another intersection—again continue straight on Trail 1199. At **11.3 miles**, arrive at yet another intersection; this time turn right, leaving White River Trail. Ride about 40 yards down to Hwy 410. Cross it, turn left, and ride up the highway. At **11.4 miles**, turn right onto Buck Creek Road and cross the White River. Find the small parking area on the left to complete the ride, **11.5 miles**.

NOTES:

_____

_____

_____

_____

Ride 45 ✪✪✪✪

SUN TOP

Distance	**21.0 miles**, loop
Terrain	Singletrack, dirt roads; brutal 7-mile road climb, some singletrack climbing, **cumulative gain: 4,500 ft.**
Duration	4 to 7 hours
Travel	61 miles from Seattle
Skill Level	Advanced
Season	Summer, early fall
Map	Green Trails: *Greenwater*
Explorability	Low
Restrictions	NW Forest Pass
More Info	Mount Baker-Snoqualmie National Forest, Snoqualmie District (Enumclaw), 360-825-6585, www.fs.fed.us/r6/mbs/

Prelude

One notch below epic, the ride to the top of Sun Top includes about seven skyscrapers worth of elevation gain and some seriously technical singletrack. And if you aren't physically and, more importantly, mentally prepared, this ride will kick your ass. But the eye-bugging views from the top, the sweet high meadows, and the corkscrewing descent make this ride a gem. Don't blow out your legs on the torturous road climb or you won't be able to truly appreciate the epic descent. Note:

The Forest Service rebuilt and rerouted sections of the Sun Top Trail, making the singletrack climb more ridable and the descent less hardscrabble.

Driving Directions

From Seattle, head east on Interstate 90, south on Interstate 405 to Exit 4, then south on State Highway 169 to Enumclaw. In Enumclaw, take State Hwy 410 south toward Mount Rainier. As you leave town, pass milepost 26 and set your odometer to zero. At 23.3 miles, just past milepost 49, turn right on Forest Road 73. Stay on the main road. At 23.7 miles, just after crossing the White River, park on the right.

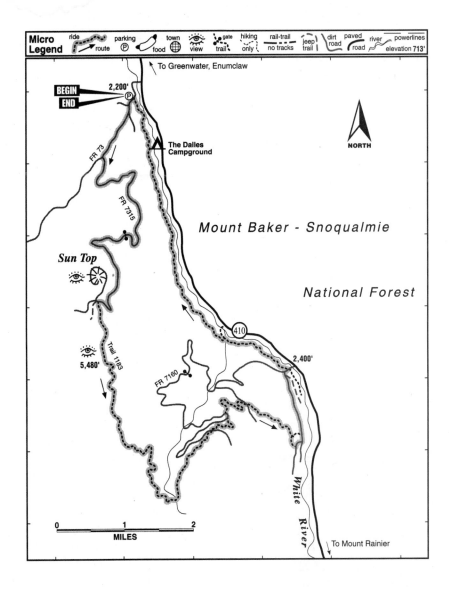

Micro Legend

ride route · parking ⓟ · town · food · view · gate trail · hiking only · rail-trail no tracks · jeep trail · dirt road · paved road · river · powerlines · elevation 713'

To Greenwater, Enumclaw

BEGIN END 2,200'

NORTH

The Dalles Campground

FR 73

FR 7315

Mount Baker - Snoqualmie

Sun Top

National Forest

5,480'

Trail 1183

410

2,400'

FR 7160

White River

0   1   2
MILES

To Mount Rainier

The Ride

From the bridge over the White River, ride up FR 73. When the road forks at **0.2 mile**, bear right, following the main road. At **0.9 mile**, turn left on FR 7315 and begin the radical climb up toward Sun Top. Without a break, the road grinds and switchbacks up the north side of the mountain. Ignore lesser spurs. At **3.0 miles,** ride straight around the gate. Around the **4.0-mile** mark, using your natural tendency to make excuses, you'll convince yourself your rear tire has gone flat. Just before a fork at **5.7 miles**, Trail 1183 crosses the road. Turn left onto this trail; the sign says, "Airstrip 8." (If you want to bag Sun Top, turn right on Trail 1183, then turn right when you reach a dirt road. From here, pedal up the road to the top, about one and a half miles away. While this spur adds 540 feet of climbing and slightly more than three miles to the distance, the views from the lookout are worth it.)

From the dirt road, Trail 1183 heads due south, ascending a ridge that actually rises higher than Sun Top. This steep trail may prove to be a hike-a-bike, but it's all ridable. Several times it seems as though you've reached the top, but it's not until the **6.9-mile** mark—**Woof!**—that the sharp ridge is tamed. The views to both the east and west are awesome. From the ridgetop, the trail traverses the precipitous east-facing slope. Open hillsides and rock escarpments give way to a thick forest as the trail drops and switchbacks downward. After a short but irritatingly steep ascent around **8.5 miles**, gravity becomes your friend once more. At **9.5 miles**, the trail elbows to the left as it crosses Buck Creek.

After a fast, fun downhill traverse, cross a road at **10.6 miles**. Reach a fork in the trail at **10.9 miles**, and bear left. At **11.2 miles**, the trail widens then narrows again. From here, the trail zigzags and switchbacks down the head of the ridge. It's smooth at first but becomes rugged and steep through a recent clearcut. The trail crosses a bermed road, **12.5 miles**. Continue down the trail on the opposite side. Reach a fork at **12.9 miles**—bear right. The way levels and winds through a thick wet forest. At **13.3 miles**, the trail crosses a jeep trail—follow the Trail sign. At **13.4**

Crossing Buck Creek on the Sun Top descent

miles, arrive at a fork and turn left. The wide trail crosses a small creek and then ends at a dirt road, **13.7 miles**—turn left. Stay on the main road as it bends to the left and then runs along the edge of an airstrip. Just past the north end of the airstrip, **15.0 miles**, reach Buck Creek Road and turn right. At **15.2 miles**, just before crossing the White River, turn left onto Skookum Flats Trail 1194. (To save a lot of time, you can skip Skookum Flats Trail and ride down Hwy 410 to FR 73.)

When the trail divides at **15.3 miles**, stay to the left. At **15.5 miles**, take the right fork, wrap around a tight turn, and cross a short bridge. From here the trail is quite technical, with awkwardly placed roots and tight turns, as it traverses a precipitous slope. Ride across a bridge at **16.3 miles**. At **16.6 miles**, arrive at a fork—bear left, away from the river. (The right fork immediately uses a suspension bridge

Ascending Trail 1183

to cross the White River and leads to Hwy 410—your last chance to bail out.) You'll curse the next one quarter-mile, as the trail climbs up steps, roots, large rocks, and a series of short wood walkways. **Woof!** The trail levels out at **16.8 miles**. At **17.0 miles**, take the right fork and traverse the bank high above the river. The next couple of miles are technical and difficult, a hike-a-bike for less skilled cyclists. Ride through stands of old growth, with limited but lovely views of the White River.

After the **19.5-mile** point, though, the trail becomes less difficult. At **20.0 miles**, reach a clearing—bear right to stay on a trail that parallels the river. From here, stay on the main trail, weaving past some gigantic Douglas firs. At **21.0 miles**, reach FR 73 and the end of the loop.

NOTES:

_____

_____

_____

_____

Ride 46 ✿✿✿

FAWN RIDGE

Distance	**11.9 miles**, loop
Terrain	Singletrack, dirt roads; tough 6-mile climb, **cumulative gain: 2,300 ft.**
Duration	2 to 3 hours
Travel	66 miles from Seattle
Skill Level	Advanced
Season	Summer, fall
Map	Green Trails: *Greenwater*
Explorability	Moderate
Restrictions	NW Forest Pass
More Info	Mount Baker-Snoqualmie National Forest, Snoqualmie District (Enumclaw), 360-825-6585, www.fs.fed.us/r6/mbs/

Prelude

Fawn Ridge is pretty much the poor man's Sun Top—similar but less epic, requiring less time and fewer preparatory workouts. The trip up Buck Creek Road and down Fawn Ridge on singletrack to the White River proves exhilarating,

View of the palisades from Fawn Ridge

beautiful, and a little bit frustrating: It's an exhilarating 2,000 foot climb (and 2,000 foot descent!), you get beautiful views of the palisades across the majestic White River valley, and it's frustrating that a panoramic vista of Mount Rainier should be part of the package and it's not. After the first mile, Buck Creek Road is lightly traveled by vehicles and never gets overly steep (unlike the Sun Top climb). The descent on Trail 1183 is rough, steep, and technical in places. It's heavily used on summer weekends, so watch out for other trail users.

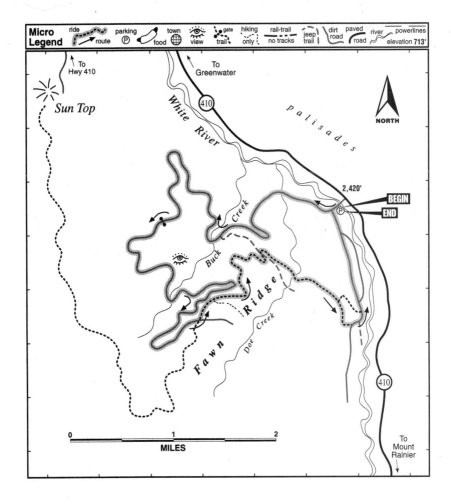

Micro Legend ride route · parking (P) · town/food · view · gate/trail · hiking only · rail-trail no tracks · jeep trail · dirt road · paved road · river · powerlines · elevation 713'

To Hwy 410

To Greenwater

Sun Top

White River

410

Palisades

NORTH

2,420'

BEGIN

END

P

Buck Creek

Ridge

Doe Creek

Fawn

410

To Mount Rainier

0 · 1 · 2

MILES

Driving Directions

From Seattle, head east on Interstate 90, south on Interstate 405 to Exit 4, then south on Highway 169 to Enumclaw. In Enumclaw, take Highway 410 south toward Mount Rainier. As you leave town, pass milepost 26 and set your odometer to zero. At 28.4 miles, just past milepost 54, turn right on Buck Creek Road. Cross over the White River and take the first left into the parking area.

The Ride

From the parking area, return to Buck Creek Road, turn left, and ride west, away from Hwy 410. When the road forks, bear right, away from the airstrip. After a long straightaway, the road bends to the left, **0.7 mile**, and begins climbing. Stay on the obvious main road. At **1.3 miles**, pass a lesser road on the left and continue up. At

First snow on Buck Creek Road

1.8 miles, pass another road on the left. Soon after, the road crosses Buck Creek and bears to the right, cutting an extended traverse up the side of the mountain and offering views of the palisades (see Ride 47) across the valley.

Follow the switchback up to the left, then ride around a gate, **3.0 miles**. Ascending steadily, the road crosses two Buck Creek tributaries and then the creek itself, before leveling somewhat around the **5.5-mile** mark. At **5.9 miles**, ignore a road that cuts down to the left. Continue up the main road. After two long switchbacks, reach Sun Top Trail 1183 at **7.4 miles**. (The road ends less than one half-mile farther.) Turn left onto the Trail 1183, and begin the headlong descent.

After a short spin through thick forest, bypass the trail to Doe Falls on the right, **7.7 miles**. Around the corner, the trail widens then narrows again. From here, the trail corkscrews down the head of Fawn Ridge, at times smooth, at times rocky and loose.

After a bunch of switchbacks through a recent clearcut, the trail crosses a road, **9.1 miles**. Continue down the trail on the opposite side. Reach a fork at **9.6 miles**— bear right. The way levels and winds through a thick wet forest. At **10.0 miles**, the trail crosses a jeep trail. Follow the Trail sign. When the trail divides again at **10.1 miles**, turn left. The wide trail crosses a small creek and then ends at a dirt road, **10.4 miles**—turn left. Stay on the main road as it bends to the left, and then traces the edge of the airstrip. Just past the airstrip, **11.7 miles**, reach Buck Creek Road. Turn right and ride back to the small parking area near Hwy 410, **11.9 miles**.

NOTES:

_____

_____

_____

_____

Ride 47 ✿✿✿✿✿

PALISADES TRAIL

Distance	**21.7 miles,** loop
Terrain	Singletrack, dirt roads; torturous 5-mile dirt road climb, lots of tough climbs on the trail, **cumulative gain: 5,100 ft.**
Duration	4 to 8 hours
Travel	69 miles from Seattle
Skill Level	Expert
Season	Summer, early fall
Maps	Green Trails: *Greenwater, Lester*
Explorability	High
Restrictions	NW Forest Pass
More Info	Mount Baker-Snoqualmie National Forest, Snoqualmie District (Enumclaw), 360-825-6585, www.fs.fed.us/r6/mbs/

Prelude

Tough, rugged, and dangerous, this incredibly beautiful ride passes through thick Douglas fir and hemlock forest, with pines here and there on the high ridge, and colorful hanging meadows along the side slopes. With Mount Rainier acting as a beacon to the west and the Norse Peak Wilderness Area stretching east, the loop couldn't be more wild or picturesque. The climb is liable to sucker-punch you, and the precipitous palisades, which fall 2,000 feet into the White River valley from the trail's edge, can produce an excellent knee-quivering vertigo. In between, you'll do some gentle noodling, some hike-a-biking, and a lot of zipping. The Snoqualmie Ranger District in Enumclaw has done well to keep this trail open to bicyclists.

Driving Directions

From Seattle, go east on Interstate 90, south on Interstate 405 to Exit 4, then south on Highway 169 to Enumclaw. In Enumclaw, take Highway 410 south. As you leave town, pass milepost 26 and zero your odometer. At 30.2 miles, just past milepost 56, turn left on Forest Road 7174 (Corral Pass Road). At 30.8 miles, stay left to remain on FR 7174. At 31.0 miles, park in the small dirt pull-out on the left.

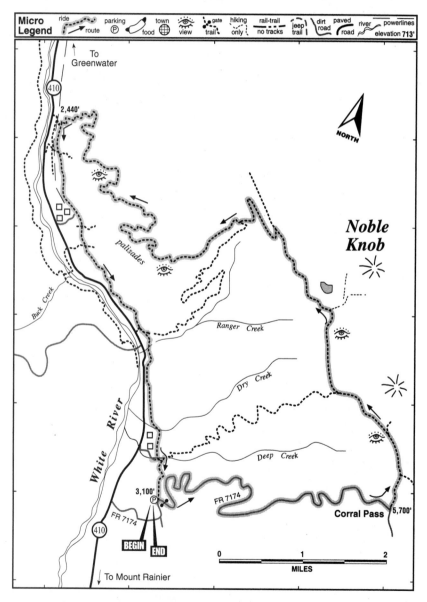

Admiring Norse Peak Wilderness

The Ride

From the gate, stick it in first gear, stare down at your front tire, and pedal up Corral Pass Road. It's a grunt. Keep an ear out for motorized vehicles and stay on the obvious main road. Ride across Sucker Flats at **3.9 miles**, then continue up. **Woof!** The road levels around the **4.5-mile** mark. At Corral Pass, **5.2 miles**, reach a T and turn left.

Find Noble Knob Trail 1184 on the right—this is your wonderland entrance. The trail is narrow to start, then widens. Reach a T at **5.8 miles**, and turn left onto a wide trail, which traverses north, following the contours of Dalles Ridge. Ignore a trail back to the right at **6.1 miles**. This stretch, atop the sparsely forested ridge, affords excellent views of Mount Rainier. Stay on the main trail, a doubletrack now, ignoring the spurs. Reach a fork at **6.7 miles** and bear left onto singletrack. After a short but steep climb to a high point along the ridge, you get great views of Norse Peak Wilderness, Mount Rainier, Mount Adams, and beyond. From here, the trail drops to an intersection at **7.1 miles**. Stay to the right on Noble Knob Trail 1184. Continue through the sparse woods, tracing an incredible traverse along the west side of Dalles Ridge.

The trail gradually ascends to a final high point, **8.0 miles**, then crosses over to the east side of the ridge and descends. Just after several short steep switchbacks, reach an intersection at **8.4 miles** and turn left onto Dalles Ridge Trail 1173. The trail's choppy and technical here, up and down then traversing this lower ridge. At **9.4 miles** the trail divides: Take the left fork down the Ranger Creek Trail 1197. The trail drops quickly, switchbacking for the next mile. At **10.6 miles**, reach a log shelter and a fork in the trail. (The left fork drops down Ranger Creek Trail. See Ride 48.) Go around the shelter to find the right-hand fork—Palisades Trail 1198.

From the shelter, ride along this narrow trail, traversing and climbing in spurts along the ridge that is Little Ranger Peak. At **11.5 miles**, reach an amazing viewpoint, looking out from the top of the palisades. Over the next three miles, the trail winds generally downhill through the woods, often dancing out to the edge of these cliffs that overlook the White River valley. The trail is loose and root-strewn, and riding along the edge of the palisades is dangerous. At **13.4 miles**, cross a bridge over a small creek, climb a short hill, then enter a clearcut. The trail crosses the clearcut and reenters the forest at **13.8 miles**.

From here the trail climbs for a short distance, drops steadily, then again pops out to the edge of the cliffs, **15.7 miles**. Shortly, the trail begins a series of switchbacks that become progressively steeper and more severe. Around **16.1 miles**, the trail funnels into a gully. Hoist your bike onto your shoulder and scramble down the stairs and rocky switchbacks for about one half-mile.

At **17.0 miles**, reach a 4-way intersection: Take a gentle left onto White River Trail 1199. Stay on White River Trail, bypassing a junction at **17.3 miles**. At **17.8 miles**, reach a clearing that marks the edge of Camp Sheppard. At **17.9 miles**, with some buildings on the right, find a trail and the Trail sign on the left. **Whoa**—this is easy to miss. The trail bears right, cutting above the buildings at Camp Sheppard. After this turn, stay on the main trail, bypassing many spurs. At **18.2 miles**, arrive at another intersection—continue straight on Trail 1199. At **18.4 miles**, reach another intersection—again continue straight on Trail 1199.

The rooted trail gradually climbs up the eastern edge of the White River valley; the roots combined with fatigue from the strenuous ride can make this a difficult section despite the modest grade. At **19.5 miles**, continue straight, ignoring a short spur down to the right to Highway 410. Just up the hill, reach a fork (the Ranger Creek Trail takes off to the left). Bear right at the fork, continuing straight on White River Trail 1199 toward Corral Pass Road. At **21.0 miles**, the trail divides upon arriving at Deep Creek. Don't cross the bridge; instead, take the left fork upstream. At **21.2 miles**, after a dismount, take the right fork and cross a wooden bridge over the creek. Pedal around a hillside, and then up a rocky trail. Reach Corral Pass Road at **21.7 miles**.

NOTES:

_____

_____

_____

_____

Ride 48 ✹✹✹✹

RANGER CREEK

Distance	**18.1 miles**, loop
Terrain	Singletrack, dirt roads; long grueling climb, some walking, steep descent, **cumulative gain: 4,100 ft.**
Duration	3 to 6 hours
Travel	69 miles from Seattle
Skill Level	Expert
Season	Summer, early fall
Maps	Green Trails: *Greenwater, Lester*
Explorability	Moderate
Restrictions	NW Forest Pass
More Info	Mount Baker-Snoqualmie National Forest, Snoqualmie District (Enumclaw), 360-825-6585, www.fs.fed.us/r6/mbs/

Prelude

The dirt road climb up Forest Road 7174 to Corral Pass is just plain torture. But the smooth trail and beautiful scenery along Dalles Ridge help eclipse the pain of the ascent. Views into adjacent Norse Peak Wilderness and across the White River valley to Mount Rainier don't hurt either. And the descent is pure Jedi.

Driving Directions

From Seattle, go east on Interstate 90, south on Interstate 405 to Exit 4, then south on Highway 169 to Enumclaw. In Enumclaw, take Highway 410 south. As you leave town, pass milepost 26 and zero your odometer. At 30.2 miles, just past milepost 56, turn left on Forest Road 7174 (Corral Pass Road). At 30.8 miles, stay left to remain on FR 7174. At 31.0 miles, park in the small pull-out on the left.

Seeing white light

The Ride

From the gate, stick it in first gear, stare down at your front tire, and pedal up Corral Pass Road. It's a grunt. Keep an ear out for motorized vehicles, and stay on the obvious main road. Ride across Sucker Flats at **3.9 miles**, then continue up. **Woof!** The road levels around the **4.5-mile** mark. At Corral Pass, **5.2 miles**, reach a T and turn left.

Running out of daylight on Dalles Ridge

Find Noble Knob Trail 1184 on the right—this is your wonderland entrance. The trail is narrow to start, then widens. Reach a T at **5.8 miles** and turn left onto a wide trail, which traverses north, following the contours of Dalles Ridge. Ignore a trail back to the right at **6.1 miles**. This stretch, atop the sparsely forested ridge, affords excellent views of Mount Rainier. Stay on the main trail, a doubletrack now, ignoring the spurs. Reach a fork at **6.7 miles** and bear left onto singletrack. After a short but steep climb to a high point along the ridge, you get great views of Norse Peak Wilderness, Mount Rainier, Mount Adams, and beyond. From here, the trail drops to an intersection at **7.1 miles**. Stay to the right on Noble Knob Trail 1184. Continue through the sparse woods, tracing an incredible traverse along the west side of Dalles Ridge.

The trail gradually ascends to a final high point, **8.0 miles**, then crosses over to the east side of the ridge and descends. Just after several short steep switchbacks, reach an intersection at **8.4 miles** and turn left onto Dalles Ridge Trail 1173. The trail's choppy and technical here, up and down then traversing this lower ridge. At **9.4 miles** the trail divides: Take the left fork down the Ranger Creek Trail 1197. The trail switchbacks down for the next mile. At **10.6 miles**, reach a log shelter and a fork in the trail—go left to continue down Ranger Creek Trail 1197. (The right prong heads out to the Palisades Trail, see Ride 47.)

The vertical drop begins immediately. The trail is so steep and rough that the next couple miles may be a hike-a-bike for some riders. At **12.9 miles**, bear to the left at the fork. From here the downward grade isn't quite as dramatic, as the trail switchbacks through a dense forest. Reach a T at **16.0 miles** and turn left. At **16.1 miles**, cross Ranger Creek. The trail climbs and descends on a tricky traverse above

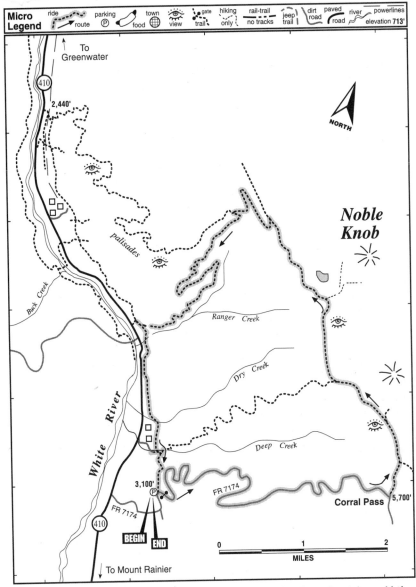

Micro Legend
ride route · parking ℗ · town food ⊕ · view 👁 · gate trail · hiking only · rail-trail no tracks · jeep trail · dirt road · paved road · river · powerlines · elevation **713'**

To Greenwater

410

2,440'

Palisades

Buck Creek

Noble Knob

Ranger Creek

Dry Creek

Deep Creek

FR 7174

White River

3,100'
℗

FR 7174

410

BEGIN **END**

Corral Pass **5,700'**

0   1   2
MILES

↓ To Mount Rainier

NORTH

Hwy 410. At **17.4 miles**, ignore a bridge across Deep Creek on the right and hike-a-bike up to a fork at **17.6 miles**. Turn right here and cross this second bridge over the creek. After more climbing and a short traverse, reach FR 7174 at **18.1 miles**.

NOTES:

Ride 49 ✻✻✻✻

CRYSTAL MOUNTAIN

Distance	**14 miles**, loop
Terrain	Singletrack, dirt roads; long trail and road climb, probably a hike-a-bike, **cumulative gain: 3,550 ft.**
Duration	3 to 5 hours
Travel	73 miles from Seattle
Skill Level	Advanced
Season	Summer, early fall
Maps	Green Trails: *Bumping Lake, Mount Rainier East*
Explorability	Moderate
Restrictions	None
More Info	Mount Baker-Snoqualmie National Forest, Snoqualmie District (Enumclaw), 360-825-6585, www.fs.fed.us/r6/mbs/

Prelude

It could be argued that one stretch of singletrack along Crystal Mountain ridge is the best trail in the state. With in-your-face views of Mount Rainier and a sweeping vista of the White River valley to the west and a series of mountain lakes and ridge crests to the east, the visual experience from this trail can't be improved upon. The trail itself, narrow and winding on a slight descent, passes through grassy meadows, with groves of fir and pine. It would be sweet if this trail went on forever. But there's one big problem with this otherwise perfect trail: It's hard to get to. You will spend hours riding short sections and then pushing your bike up toward the top of the mountain to reach that short section of singletrack nirvana. Note that rather than taking the long arduous trail up to the top, some prefer the more direct (though still difficult) route up the dirt roads from the base of the ski area to the top.

Driving Directions

From Seattle, go east on Interstate 90, south on Interstate 405 to Exit 4, then south on Highway 169 to Enumclaw. In Enumclaw, take Highway 410 south. As you leave town, pass milepost 26 and zero your odometer. At 31.5 miles, just past milepost 57 but before entering Mount Rainier National Park, turn left on Crystal Mountain Blvd. At 35.5 miles, just after the road levels out, park in a wide, unmarked pull-off on the right.

The Ride

From the car, pedal up Crystal Mountain Road for a short distance, then cross the road to Forest Road 7190-410 on the opposite side. Bypass the Norse Creek Trail, and immediately begin climbing. Traverse up the hill, paralleling Crystal Mountain Road, which is below on the right. As the road makes a hairpin turn up to the left, three trails exit on the right, **2.3 miles**. Take the middle one, Silver Creek Trail. The trail, narrow at times, wide at others, soon crosses an open ski slope.

At **2.6 miles**, turn right, away from the jeep trail and onto a singletrack. One quarter-mile farther, the trail enters the woods as it crosses a bridge. Just across the bridge, you'll find an old mine carved into the rock on the left. From here, Silver Creek Trail 1192 traverses up toward the head of the valley at a stiff rate. Between

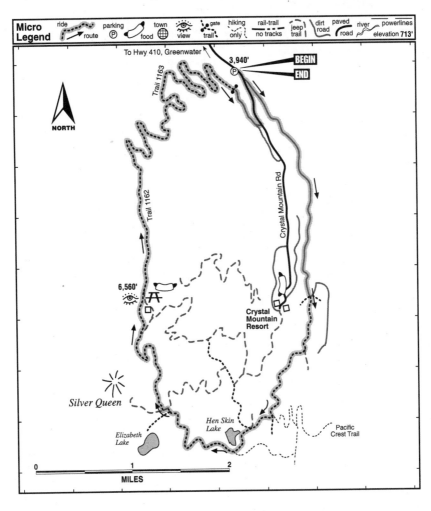

3.0 miles and **3.6 miles**, many pitches of the trail may mandate walking. Reach a 4-way intersection at **3.6 miles**, and switchback right toward Hen Skin Lake. At **4.1 miles**, arrive at a fork above Crystal Mountain's Chair 4—turn left on the wide trail.

Arrive at Hen Skin Lake, **4.2 miles**. Keep the lake on your right, ignoring the many desire paths, and upon reaching the far end climb away from the lake (and the bugs!). The trail is rough and technical in many spots. Climb past Miners Lakes, passing the first at **4.5 miles** and the second at **4.8 miles**. Reach a fork at **5.1 miles**: Bear right, cross the little creek, reach a jeep road, and turn left. Ride up the steep road about 200 yards and find a singletrack—take it. **Whoa**—this is a little tricky, so take your time. Pass under two chairlifts and by a couple of dirt roads.

The trail traverses up a steep gravelly slope, then switchbacks up to a saddle, **6.4 miles**. Continue up and around, then at a dirt road take the trail on the left that cuts up a steep traverse behind the top of the mountain. Turn right on the dirt road near the top, **6.6 miles**. **Woof!** At **6.7 miles**, reach the top of the chairlift, with the summit house 50 yards to the right. (When it's open for business, you can buy cheeseburgers here and admire the panoramic view while you eat.)

To continue the ride, turn left, away from the summit house, and ride north along the ridgetop road toward a chairlift on the opposite side of the bowl. Ride behind (to the west) the chairlift on a wide trail. Here begins the beautiful ridgetop traverse. Stay on the main trail. Pass beyond the Crystal Mountain boundary, **7.6 miles**. At a fork, **7.9 miles**, go left. The trail soon begins switchbacking from one side of the ridge to the other, before dropping down to the east toward Crystal Mountain Road. **Whoa**—watch out for equestrians on the descent.

After a long series of switchbacks, reach a dirt parking area, **12.9 miles**. Ride out the dirt road to Crystal Mountain Road and turn left. Ride down the road to the small pull-off on the left at **14.0 miles**.

NOTES:

_____

_____

_____

_____

Ride 50 ✹✹

WESTSIDE ROAD

Distance	**19 miles**, out and back
Terrain	Dirt road; long climb, never too steep, **cumulative gain: 3,600 ft.**
Duration	3 to 4 hours
Travel	85 miles from Seattle
Skill Level	Beginner
Season	Summer, early fall
Map	Trail Illustrated: *Mount Rainier National Park*
Explorability	Low
Restrictions	Mount Rainier National Park entrance fee, no dogs
More Info	Mount Rainier National Park, 360-569-2211, www.nps.gov/mora/

Prelude

When Mount Rainier's Westside Road washed out, the Park Service decided to gate it and not worry about the maintenance any longer. That's a good thing for bicyclists because until the Park Service allows bikes on dirt trails, gated dirt roads are the best we can hope for. Several trails, now "remote" due to the washout, begin from this road, making a bike-and-hike trip something to consider. The road makes it easy riding, but given the stout elevation gain, this is a difficult two-wheel ride.

Driving Directions

From Renton, go south on Highway 167 to Puyallup. Take Highway 512 east for a short distance before heading south on Highway 161. South of Eatonville, turn left on Highway 7 toward Elbe. In Elbe, stay left toward Mount Rainier, now following Highway 706. After 10 miles, enter Mount Rainier National Park. Pass Sunshine Point Campground on the right, then take the first left on Westside Road. Drive about 3 miles to a gate. Park here.

The Ride

From the gate, pedal up Westside Road. The first one half-mile, over loose rocks, demands some technical bike-handling skills, but the re-

Stream crossing on Westside Road

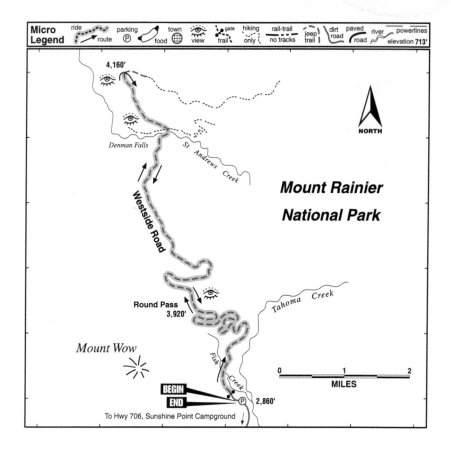

Micro Legend: ride · route · parking ⓟ · town · food ⊕ · gate · view · hiking trail · only · rail-trail / no tracks · jeep trail · dirt road · paved road · river · powerlines · elevation 713'

4,160'

Denman Falls

St Andrews Creek

Mount Rainier National Park

NORTH

Westside Road

Round Pass 3,920'

Tahoma Creek

Mount Wow

Fish Creek

0   1   2
MILES

BEGIN
END   2,860'

To Hwy 706, Sunshine Point Campground

mainder of the road is smooth, and the riding easy. After a healthy climb, pedal around a sweeping turn in the road, **2.25 miles**. Stay on the main road. From the crest of Round Pass at **3.2 miles**, check out the excellent views of Mount Rainier. You'll find a Marine Memorial here (for a plane that crashed nearby during WWII).

From the memorial, the road descends quickly. Begin climbing again at **6.4 miles**. At **8.25 miles**, cross a bridge. Immediately after the bridge, find the trail to Denman Falls on the left. It's worth the quarter-mile hike to the falls. Continuing up, reach Klapatche Point and the end of the road at **9.5 miles**. Check out the remarkable vista down into the Puyallup River valley. After a picnic here, turn around and retrace your route to the parking area, **19.0 miles**.

NOTES:

_____

_____

Destination 51 ✿✿✿✿

PORTER CREEK

Distance	**22 miles**, loop
Terrain	Singletrack, dirt roads; steep climbs, lots of hike-a-bike
Duration	4 to 8 hours
Travel	92 miles from Seattle
Skill Level	Expert
Season	Summer, fall
Map	Department of Natural Resources: *Capitol Forest*
Explorability	High
More Info	Washington State Department of Natural Resources, Central Region, 360-748-2383, www.wa.gov/dnr/

Prelude

Known during much of the 1990s as the Love-Hate Loop, this Capitol Forest route now offers a lot more sorrow than joy, and that's why it's not a full ride in *Kissing the Trail* any longer. It is still traversable (you masochist, you), and if you want the details, send a note to Adventure Press (POB 14059, Seattle, WA 98114). Suffice it to say, you are happy you aren't spending a day in hell at Porter Creek. It was a challenging loop worth all the effort (and the long drive). However, nip and tuck logging operations and lack of trail maintenance have left this trail hardscrabble, overgrown, obliterated in places, and downright miserable. Of course, there are a few sections of perfect singletrack left, and that's the real shame of it.

Driving Directions

From Seattle, take Interstate 5 south to Exit 104 near Olympia. Take Highway 101 West, then bear left on Highway 8 toward Aberdeen. Just before Elma, turn left on Hwy 12 toward Rochester, and zero out your odometer. At 6.0 miles, in the hamlet of Porter, turn left onto Porter Creek Road, following the signs to Porter Creek Campground. At 9.1 miles, reach a fork and bear left. At a 4-way intersection, 9.5 miles, go straight (an easy left) onto B-Line, following the campground signs. Drive through the campground and park in a pull-out on the right, 10.5 miles.

NOTES:

_____

_____

Ride 52 ✿✿✿✿

MIMA CREEK

Distance	**21.7 miles**, loop
Terrain	Singletrack; relentless climbing, **cumulative gain: 3,050 ft.**
Duration	3 to 7 hours
Travel	71 miles from Seattle
Skill Level	Advanced
Season	Late spring, summer, fall
Map	Department of Natural Resources: *Capitol Forest*
Explorability	High
Restrictions	None
More Info	Washington State Department of Natural Resources, Central Region, 360-748-2383, www.wa.gov/dnr/

Prelude

Just south of Puget Sound, Capitol Forest contains one of the most extensive trail systems in the region, and it's all open to mountain biking, much of it quite rigorous. The loose rocky trails, muddy bogs, and sharp hills on this ride demand a full supply of both stamina and riding skill. But the beautiful lush forest and out-and-out adventure of it all make the hills seem more like minor nuisances than lung-busters. Like the Porter Creek loop (see Destination 51), Mima Creek is located on the nonmotorized side of Capitol Forest. You won't be bothered by engines, but you will have to contend with trails chopped up and puréed by horse hooves. Ride with care as hikers, runners, and equestrians use these trails extensively.

Driving Directions

From Seattle, take Interstate 5 to Exit 95 south of Olympia. The exit ramp wraps around to Highway 121. Set your odometer to zero when you reach Hwy 121, then turn left (west) toward Littlerock. At 3.0 miles, pass through Littlerock, following signs to Capitol Forest. At 3.8 miles, reach a T and turn right. At 6.3 miles, just after entering Capitol Forest, pull into Margaret McKenny Campground on the left. Take note of a trail on the right immediately after entering, but proceed straight. Take the second left to find the day-use parking and equestrian staging area.

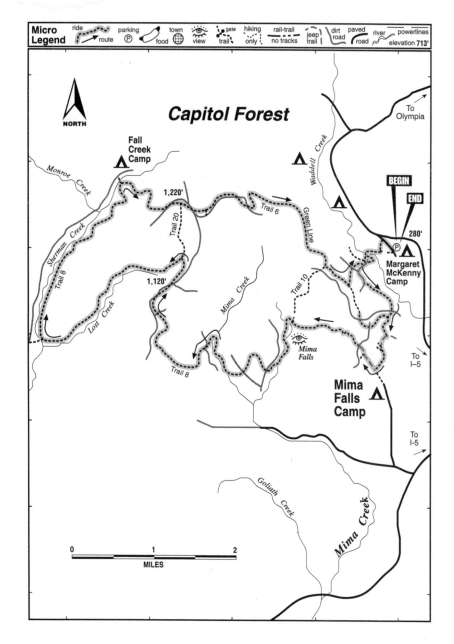

Micro Legend

ride route · parking ⓟ · town/food · view · gate trail · hiking only · rail-trail no tracks · jeep trail · dirt road · paved road · river · powerlines · elevation 713'

Capitol Forest

NORTH

Fall Creek Camp

Monroe Creek

Sherman Creek

1,220'

Trail 20

1,120'

Trail 8

Lost Creek

Trail 6

Green Line

Mima Creek

Waddell Creek

To Olympia

BEGIN

END

280'

ⓟ Margaret McKenny Camp

Trail 10

Mima Falls

To I-5

Mima Falls Camp

To I-5

Goliath Creek

Mima Creek

0   1   2
MILES

The Ride

From the parking area, ride back toward the campground entrance and find the Green Line 6 and Trail 8 access trail. Stay on the main trail—ignoring spurs—as you wind down to Waddell Creek, **0.3 mile**. At creekside, bear right and pedal for

Near Mima Falls on Trail 8

a short distance to a bridge, **0.4 mile**. Cross the bridge and ride up the trail on the opposite bank. The trail switchbacks up to a fork—turn right (passing the "DO NOT ENTER" trail on the left). Pedal up a steep hill to a road at **0.6 mile**. Ignore a singletrack back to the right just prior to the road. Ignore another trail straight across the road. Turn right onto the road. At **0.65 mile**, ignore yet another trail on the right. When the road divides at **0.7 mile**, bear left and ascend. At **0.8 mile**, find the Waddell Loop Trail on the left and take it.

At **1.5 mile**, cross a gravel road and continue down the beautiful trail on the opposite side. Ignore a trail back on the right at **1.6 miles**. When the trail splits again, turn right, riding away from the Firearms Impact Area. At **1.8 miles**, bypass two trails on the right and continue ascending gently through a clearcut on a loose trail. At **2.2 miles**, reach a T at Green Line Trail 6 and turn right on Mima-Porter Trail 8. At **2.4 miles**, cross a road. The trail narrows. At **2.8 miles**, bypass a lesser trail on the right. Cross over a bridge at **2.9 miles**. Ignore a trail on the right at **3.1 miles**. When the trail forks at **3.8 miles**, go left (the right fork is Trail 10). Just after a bridge at **3.9 miles**, reach a fork and bear left.

Arrive at Mima Falls, **4.2 miles**. At **4.7 miles**, after a downhill traverse to a bridge and a short climb, reach a road. Continue on the trail across the road. The trail crosses another road at **5.1 miles**. From here, a long grueling hill begins. Ride straight across another road to the trail on the opposite side, **6.2 miles**. The climbing and switchbacking continue up to **7.3 miles**, where the trail levels somewhat. Stay on the main trail, ignoring the short spur roads. At **7.8 miles**, ride across another road to the trail opposite. At a 4-way intersection, **8.2 miles**, continue straight on the main trail.

At **9.4 miles**, reach an intersection of gravel roads—D-4000 and D-5000. Find the trail diagonally across the intersection. At a fork in the trail, **9.9 miles**, turn left, staying on Mima-Porter Trail 8. (A right turn onto Trail 20 shortens the ride by 7 miles; pick up the ride again at the 17.4-mile mark when Trail 20 intersects with Green Line Trail 6.) From the intersection, the rocky trail descends along Lost Creek to its confluence with Sherman Creek at **11.5 miles**. Just before Sherman Creek, the trail divides—turn right, riding up Sherman Creek on Mima-Porter Trail 8. The trail up Sherman Creek changes from smooth to muddy to rocky, crossing numerous bridges in various states of repair.

At **14.4 miles**, reach the junction with Green Line Trail 6. Turn right onto Trail 6, toward the McKenny Camp. (Fall Creek Camp sits across Sherman Creek to the left.) From here, the climbing begins in earnest. Cross a road to the trail on the other side, **16.4 miles**. Pass Trail 20 on the right at **16.6 miles**—stay on Trail 6, left. At **16.9 miles**, cross a road. At **17.1 miles**, ignore a trail off to the right; stay on the singletrack. At **17.4 miles**, the trail parallels a gravel road then drifts away from it. Cross gravel roads at **17.8 miles** and **18.0 miles**. From here the route drops quickly down a very rough trail.

At **20.2 miles**, a gravel road marks the junction of Trail 6 and Trail 10. Turn left just before the road, to remain on Green Line Trail 6 toward McKenny Camp. When the trail forks at **20.6 miles**, turn left onto Trail 6A. At **20.8 miles**, cross a dirt road. At **21.1 miles**, ignore a trail on the left then immediately cross a road to the trail opposite. Things should look familiar. When the trail forks at **21.2 miles**, bear right and descend to Waddell Creek. From the creek, ride up the access trail to the McKenny Camp parking area, **21.7 miles**.

NOTES:

_____

_____

_____

_____

Ride 53 ⊗⊗

BLAKE ISLAND STATE PARK

Distance	**3.9 miles**, loop
Terrain	Wide dirt trails; rolling hills, some walking, **cumulative gain: 500 ft.**
Duration	1 hour
Travel	30 minutes from Seattle by boat
Skill Level	Intermediate
Season	Year round
Map	*Blake Island State Park* map
Explorability	Moderate
Restrictions	Dogs on leash
More Info	Washington State Parks, 360-902-8844, www.parks.wa.gov

Prelude

According to some sources, Chief Seattle was born on Blake Island. Years later, in 1900, Bill Trimble bought the island and built a large estate that is now gone. Once again Blake Island is wild and undisturbed, taking a cue from its favorite son. The island's perimeter trail, wide and hilly, provides some limited but magical views of Puget Sound and the surrounding islands. The only problem is getting there.

Driving Directions

Blake Island is accessible only by boat. Either **(1)** commandeer a friend who has a boat, or **(2)** take one of the boats that depart Seattle for the Tillicum Village salmon feasts on Blake Island (March through October). Bicycles are permitted on the tour boats. For more information, call 206-933-8600 (www.tillicumvillage.com).

Celebrating a successful circuit around Blake Island

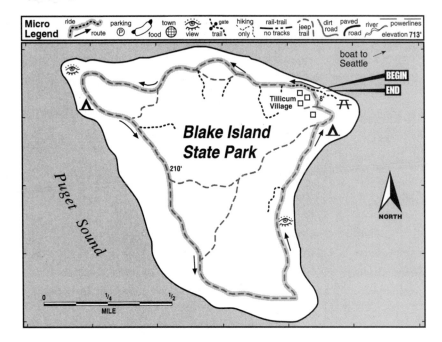

The Ride

From the marina, find the trail below the buildings that follows the shoreline counterclockwise around the island. The trail soon widens. At **0.1 mile**, bypass a trail on the left. At **0.2 mile**, pass another trail on the left. At **0.4 mile**, stay on the main road. The road divides at **0.6 mile**—take the right fork that drops down toward the water. When the roads reconnect, **1.0 mile**, continue straight. At **1.1 miles**, the road forks again—take the right fork toward the water.

At **1.25 miles**, reach a small campground on the northwest shore of Blake Island. At **1.3 miles**, turn up to the left, away from the beach. At the bathrooms, **1.4 miles**, bear to the right, continuing up. Well above the shoreline, find the road that continues around the island. **Whoa**—careful route-finding is necessary here. At **1.6 miles**, the road divides; again take the right fork. You may have to walk up several short but steep hills along this stretch. At **1.7 miles**, the road forks—take the right fork. At **2.0 miles**, take the right fork. After **2.5 miles**, take a right at the fork, heading down. Pass a beach access, then climb steadily, rounding the south end of the island. At **3.5 miles**, continue down the main road. Follow the main road through the camp area, then around the field to the marina, **3.9 miles**.

NOTES:

_____

_____

Ride 54 ✿✿✿

GREEN MOUNTAIN

Distance	**9.2 miles**, out and back
Terrain	Singletrack; long hard climb to top, **cumulative gain: 1,700 ft.**
Duration	2 to 4 hours
Travel	13 miles from Bremerton (plus 1-hour ferry ride from Seattle)
Skill Level	Intermediate
Season	Year round
Map	Department of Natural Resources: *Green Mountain*
Explorability	Moderate
Restrictions	None
More Info	Washington State Department of Natural Resources, South Puget Sound Region, 360-825-1631, www.wa.gov/dnr/

Prelude

Green Mountain State Forest, just north of Tahuya State Forest (see Ride 55, 56, 57), contains less overall acreage and just one-tenth the trail miles of Tahuya. But don't knock the 20 miles of Green Mountain singletrack. Since 20 miles isn't much for the motorcyclists, you'll find fewer of them roaming the trails here. The differences between the two state forests don't end there. While Tahuya has a rolling, generally flat topography, the Wildcat Trail to the top of Green Mountain, with an 1,100-foot cumulative elevation gain, requires focused spinning and a small chain ring. From the top on a clear day, views of the Olympics to the west and Puget Sound to the east are remarkable and worth the lung-busting effort. As with Tahuya, the Department of Natural Resources encourages mountain bike recreation here. Some of the foresters even ride mountain bikes themselves!

Driving Directions

From Seattle, take the Bremerton ferry. From Bremerton, follow Highway 304 west to Highway 3. Turn right on Hwy 3, heading northbound to Chico. Take the Chico Exit, set your odometer to zero at the end of the ramp, and turn left onto Chico Way. At 0.6 mile, turn right onto Northlake Way. At 1.0 mile, bear right onto Seabeck Highway. At 4.1 miles, turn left onto Holly Road. At 6.1 miles, find Green Mountain's Wildcat Trailhead on the left. (You can also drive around through Tacoma.)

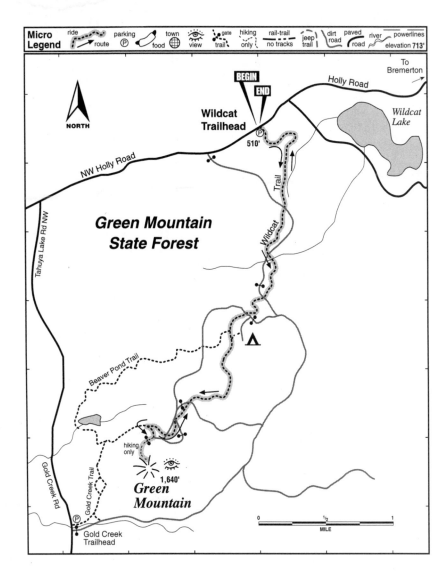

The Ride

From the gravel parking area at the trailhead, ride out Wildcat Trail. The wide trail rolls and winds through woods. Cross a dirt road at **0.9 mile**. From here, the climbing begins, and parts of the next stretch will probably have to be walked due to the steep slope and ragged trail. At **1.3 miles**, crest a hill, pass a bench, and descend on switchbacks to a dirt road. Cross the road, **1.5 miles**, and continue on the trail. After a bridge crossing, the climbing resumes.

Wildcat Trail on the way to Green Mountain summit

At **1.8 miles**, cross a dirt road and continue up the trail. At **2.1 miles**, cross another dirt road and again continue up (Green Mountain Campground is just down the road to the left). After the road crossing, the trail is steep for a pitch. After a short descent, ignore the trail on the left to the campground and continue climbing. Soon afterward, enjoy views of Puget Sound as you traverse the upper end of Lost Creek drainage. After a rocky section, the trail seems to end at a dirt road, **3.7 miles**. Turn right on the road and then immediately take the trail on the left, ascending quickly.

At **3.9 miles**, reach a 3-way intersection of gravel roads. Find the trail that exits the intersection between the two roads on the left. After another tough climb, the trail crosses a gravel road and continues on the opposite side, **4.1 miles**. From here, the trail drops through darker woods to a fork at **4.3 miles**. Take a sharp left onto Vista Trail (the right fork—straight—is the Beaver Pond Trail, which makes a nice loop). Reach the parking area near the top at **4.6 miles**. Leave your bike here and take the hiker-only trail to the summit of Green Mountain, one quarter-mile away. When you finish enjoying the view, hike back to the parking area and ride headlong back to the Wildcat Trailhead, **9.2 miles**. Watch for other users on the descent.

NOTES:

_____

_____

_____

_____

Ride 55 ❎❎❎

NORTHWEST PASSAGE

Distance	**9.8 miles**, loop
Terrain	Wide and narrow trails; constantly rolling, **cumulative gain: 550 ft.**
Duration	2 to 4 hours
Travel	18 miles from Bremerton (plus 1-hour ferry ride from Seattle)
Skill Level	Intermediate
Season	Year round
Map	Department of Natural Resources: *Tahuya State Forest*
Explorability	Extreme
Restrictions	None
More Info	Washington State Department of Natural Resources, South Puget Sound Region, 360-825-1631, www.wa.gov/dnr/

Prelude

Since the first edition of *Kissing the Trail*, the major trunk trails at Tahuya State Forest have widened by 25 percent. These trails have long had the whoops, filled with water eight months a year, but motorcycles have widened and lowered the trails, and a loose, rocky, unpredictable tread is now the norm. Meanwhile, lots of narrow singletrack has been etched in, some of it rocky, loose, and challenging riding, some of it smooth and zippy, all with fewer motorcycles. This route hits a little bit of that newer singletrack. For this reason, I used the delete key on the long Tahuya State Forest loop of earlier editions, and I added this ride along with Stimson Creek (see Ride 56).

Driving Directions

From the ferry dock in Bremerton, follow the cars to the junction of Washington Avenue and Burwell Street. Zero out your odometer here and turn left onto Burwell, a.k.a. Highway 304 West. At 1.4 miles, turn left to remain on Hwy 304. At 3.0 miles, bear left and head south on Hwy 3. At 5.2 miles, bear right, continuing on Hwy 3 toward Belfair. At 13.3 miles, turn right onto N.E. Cliffton Lane, which is Hwy 300. Stay on Hwy 300 toward Belfair State Park and Tahuya. At 16.5 miles, pass Belfair State Park on the left. At 17 miles, turn right onto Belfair-Tahuya Road. At 18.2 miles, find Mission Creek Trailhead on the right and park in the gravel lot.

The Ride

Lots of official and unofficial trails exit from the parking area at Mission Creek Trailhead. To start out on the right one, head to the back of the parking area and find the trail signs near the kiosk. A wide, loose trail begins here that leads to both Mission Creek Trail and Tahuya River Trail. At **0.1 mile**, reach a fork and go left on Tahuya River Trail, which is wide, loose, and rocky. The trail crosses dirt roads at **0.2 mile** and **0.7 mile**. At **0.8 mile**, find Northwest Passage Trail on the right and take it. Pedal out across a clearcut here. Reach a T at **1.2 miles** and turn left. Ignore the road immediately on the right. A few pedal strokes farther, hop on Northwest Passage Trail on the right.

Across clearcut toward the Northwest Passage

The trail winds back into second-growth forest. When the trail forks at **1.6 miles**, take the right prong. From here it's winding and fun, with lots of salal lining the trail. At **1.9 miles**, bear left at the fork. At **2.0 miles**, reach a fork and go right. When you hit a dirt road at **2.3 miles**, turn left. The trail winds and then climbs steeply. **Whoa**—at the top of the hill, **2.7 miles**, take a hard, easily-missed right. At **2.75 miles**, bear right again at the fork. The Northwest Passage Trail ends at **3.1 miles** when it meets Mission Creek Trail—turn left and descend. Reach a fork at **3.2 miles** and turn right, continuing on Mission Creek Trail (Connector Trail is the left fork). At **3.6 miles**, reach a fork and bear right. When the trail forks again, **3.8 miles**, bear right on Derailleur II.

After a short noodle, the trail shoots out fast and straight through a hemlock forest packed with salal and rhododendron. At **4.3 miles**, arrive at a fork and bear right. Enter a clearcut and, at **4.5 miles**, ignore a faint trail on the left. From here the trail, trenched out and lousy with loose rocks, drops precipitously down the bank. But the trail soon levels out and veers left. At **4.8 miles**, ignore a trail back

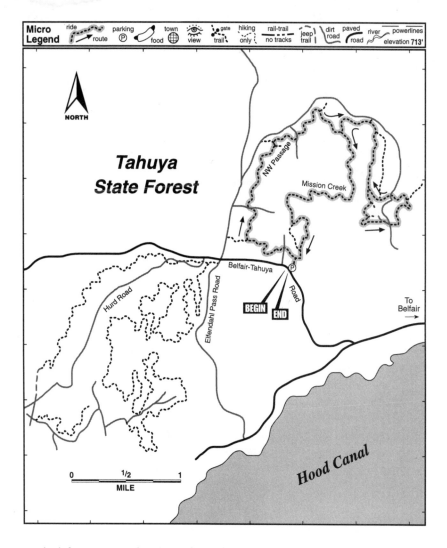

on the left. Meet a road at **4.9 miles** and bear right onto it. Immediately ignore a spur road on the right. At **5.0 miles**, reach a T in the road. Find the singletrack that exits this intersection on the opposite side—this is the continuation of Derailleur II. You re-enter the woods here, following the narrow, brushy trail as it winds upward. At **5.3 miles**, reach a T at Mission Creek Trail and go left. Cross a dirt road at **5.6 miles**. At **5.8 miles**, reach a fork and bear left, back onto Derailleur II. When the trail forks at **5.9 miles**, turn right. You should recognize this fast straight section from two miles earlier. At **6.5 miles**, reach Mission Creek Trail again and turn left. Reach a fork at **6.6 miles** and bear left. Ignore the Connector Trail on the right at

Trying out some of that motorcycle speed

7.0 miles. Bypass Northwest Passage Trail on the right at **7.1 miles**.

From here, the wide Mission Creek Trail noodles through the forest, whoops, loose rocks, motorcycles and all. At **7.9 miles**, reach a fork and stay to the right (the left fork heads down 1.9 Mile Trail and loops back to Mission Creek Trail at the 8.2-mile mark, if you're interested). Reach a dirt road at **8.1 miles**—jog to the right and regain the trail on the opposite side. At **8.2 miles**, reach a fork and stay to the right. Cross a dirt road at **8.5 miles**. At **8.7 miles**, pass Knoble Trail on the right. At **8.9 miles**, ignore two trails on the right in quick succession. When the trail divides at **9.1 miles**, turn left on Stoffer Trail. Pedal the narrow twisties as Stoffer Trail loops around to meet back up with Mission Creek Trail at **9.7 miles**—turn left. A few crank rotations farther and you'll reach the junction of Mission Creek Trail and Tahuya River Trail. Bear left here and roll in to Mission Creek Trailhead at **9.8 miles**.

NOTES:

_____

_____

_____

_____

Ride 56 ✪✪✪✪

STIMSON CREEK

Distance	**14.2 miles**, loop
Terrain	Rocky, brushy trails, dirt roads; rolling hills, **cumulative gain: 750 ft.**
Duration	3 to 6 hours
Travel	18 miles from Bremerton (plus 1-hour ferry ride from Seattle)
Skill Level	Advanced
Season	Year round
Map	Department of Natural Resources: *Tahuya State Forest*
Explorability	Extreme
Restrictions	None
More Info	Washington State Department of Natural Resources, South Puget Sound Region, 360-825-1631, www.wa.gov/dnr/

Prelude

Be forewarned: With all the ups and downs, twists and turns, overgrown trail, and less-than-perfect tread, this is a difficult ride, despite the modest distance and elevation gain. It's not my first choice for a day out on the trail. But when the high country is snowed in and you want to explore someplace new (explore being the operative term here since this route is off the Tahuya State Forest map), here's a 14-mile chunk of the 200 miles of trails at Tahuya.

Driving Directions

From the ferry dock in Bremerton, follow the cars to the junction of Washington Avenue and Burwell Street. Zero out your odometer here and turn left onto Burwell, a.k.a. Highway 304 West. At 1.4 miles, turn left to remain on Hwy 304. At 3.0 miles, bear left and head south on Hwy 3. At 5.2 miles, bear right, continuing on Hwy 3 toward Belfair. At 13.3 miles, turn right onto N.E. Cliffton Lane, which is Hwy 300. Stay on Hwy 300 toward Belfair State Park and Tahuya. At 16.5 miles, pass Belfair State Park on the left. At 17 miles, turn right onto Belfair-Tahuya Road. At 18.2 miles, find Mission Creek Trailhead on the right and park in the gravel lot.

The Ride

From the small dirt pulloff at the intersection of Belfair-Tahuya Road and Elfendahl Pass Road, take the unmarked trail that exits from the southwest corner. Cross a bridge and immediately begin climbing up a narrow trail. At **0.1 mile**, reach a fork and bear left. The trail becomes wide, and you'll hit a series of whoops, which fill with water in wet weather. When the way forks at **0.4 mile**, stay to the right on the lesser trail. At **0.5 mile**, the main trail joins your lesser trail from the left. The tread, rocky and loose, often makes for more difficult riding than expected, and sometimes brushy trail makes for a stickier, more spider-webby experience, too.

At **1.6 miles**, bear left to continue on the main trail. Reach a T at **1.7 miles** and turn left. Reach another T at **2.0 miles**, and this time turn right. At **2.5 miles**, meet up with a wide trail, then cut left onto a singletrack. At **3.2 miles**, reach a fork and bear right. Soon after the fork, the trail meanders into a clearcut. At **3.8 miles**, meet a road—jog left to find the trail again. Ignore two faint trails on the right around the **4.1-mile** mark. Reach a fork at **4.3 miles** and go left. Reach another fork at **4.7**

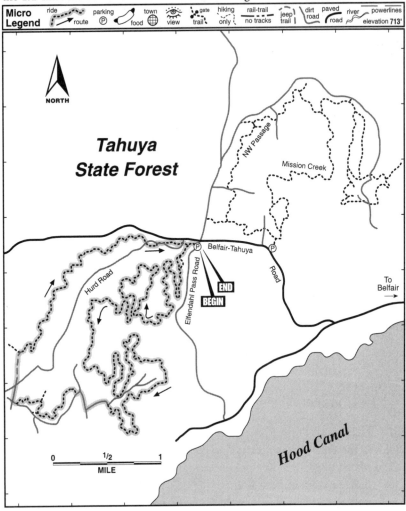

miles and again go left. Cross a dirt road at **5.4 miles**, then cross another road at **5.6 miles**, each time continuing on Trail HR UB1. At **6.1 miles**, merge with an old doubletrack and bear left.

The trail, through second-growth forest thick with salal and rhododendron, runs somewhat more smoothly here. After a sustained run, the trail crosses a road at a 5-way intersection of three roads and two trails at **7.5 miles**. Corkscrew down to a dirt road at **7.8 miles** and turn right. Ride along the road to the **8.1-mile** mark where you'll find a singletrack on the left—take it. When you pop out at the road again at **8.2 miles**, turn left. Stay on the main road here, ignoring a doubletrack on the right. At **8.4 miles**, find a trail on the left and take it.

Salal, rocks, full concentration

Riding through an old clearcut now, open and exposed, reach a bermed out road at **8.6 miles** and bear left. At **8.7 miles**, the trail veers to the right, leaving the road. (Continue down the road a very short distance to find a view of Hood Canal.)

The trail ends at a road at **9.0 miles**—go left. When the road divides at **9.1 miles**, stay to the left. Reach a T at **9.4 miles** and go right, continuing on the main road. At **9.7 miles**, reach a fork and turn left. Immediately find Trail Hurd UB1 on the right. The trail drops for a short distance, then levels. Reach a fork at **9.9 miles** and go left, then immediately turn right before reaching a dirt road. Ignore a trail on the right at **10.1 miles**. At **10.6 miles**, reach a T and turn left. When the trail forks at **10.8 miles**, go left again. At **10.9 miles**, the trail ends at a road—turn right. Arrive at a white gate and a 4-way intersection of roads—turn right. Reach another 4-way at **11.0 miles** and proceed straight, riding around the huge berm and along the edge of a clearcut.

When the road divides at **11.1 miles**, stay to the right. At **11.2 miles**, the road narrows as it leaves the clearcut—bear left. Reach a T at **11.3 miles** and turn right, descending on a lively singletrack. Drop to a bridge and then climb. At **12.1 miles** reach a fork and stay to the right on the main trail. You're back in the open again and at **12.3 miles**, when the trail ends at a narrow dirt road lined with scotch broom, turn right. Find a singletrack on the left at **12.4 miles** and take it. At **13.1 miles**, reach a fork and bear left. When the trail kisses a road on the left, stay on the trail. Cross a dirt road at **13.7 miles**. At **14.0 miles**, reach a fork and bear left. Arrive back at Elfendahl Pass Road at **14.2 miles**.

NOTES:

Ride 57 ✿ ✿ ✿

HOWELL LAKE

Distance	**7.6 miles**, loop
Terrain	Dirt trails; rolling hills, some steep, **cumulative gain: 500 ft.**
Duration	1 to 3 hours
Travel	23 miles from Bremerton (plus 1-hour ferry ride from Seattle)
Skill Level	Intermediate
Season	Year round
Map	Department of Natural Resources: *Tahuya State Forest*
Explorability	Moderate
Restrictions	None
More Info	Washington State Department of Natural Resources, South Puget Sound Region, 360-825-1631, www.wa.gov/dnr/

Prelude

The moderate Howell Lake loop sits at the western edge of Tahuya State Forest. The wide trail rolls up and down on a 7-mile circuit around Collins Lake (which you never see) beginning and ending at Howell Lake Camp and Picnic Area. Parts of the trail are somewhat technical—loose rocks, wet roots—and you may have to dismount a few times. Despite that, this is a good ride for any ambitious beginner.

Driving Directions

From the ferry dock in Bremerton, follow the cars to the junction of Washington Avenue and Burwell Street. Zero out your odometer here and turn left onto Burwell, a.k.a. Highway 304 West. At 1.4 miles, turn left to remain on Hwy 304. At 3.0 miles, bear left and head south on Hwy 3. At 5.2 miles, bear right, continuing on Hwy 3 toward Belfair. At 13.3 miles, turn right onto N.E. Cliffton Lane, which is Hwy 300. Stay on Hwy 300 toward Belfair State Park and Tahuya. At 16.5 miles, pass Belfair State Park on the left. At 17 miles, turn right onto Belfair-Tahuya Road. At 21.2 miles, turn left, to remain on Belfair-Tahuya Road. At 22.9 miles, find Howell Lake Camp and Picnic Area on the left.

The Ride

Howell Lake Trail crosses the gravel entrance road to the camp and picnic area about fifty yards from Belfair-Tahuya Road. From the picnic area, ride back up the entrance road and turn left onto the trail, riding the loop clockwise. At **0.25 mile**,

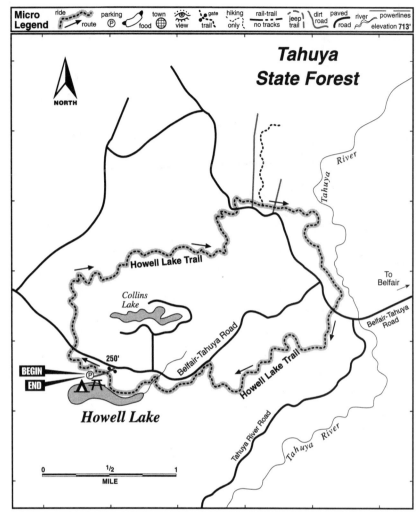

Tahuya State Forest

NORTH

Tahuya River

Howell Lake Trail

Collins Lake

To Belfair

Belfair-Tahuya Road

Howell Lake Trail

250'

BEGIN

END

Howell Lake

Tahuya River Road

Tahuya River

0   1/2   1
MILE

ignore a trail on the left. At **0.4 mile**, pass a jeep trail on the right. Just down the hill, cross Belfair-Tahuya Road. Almost immediately after the crossing, take a right at the fork. From here, stay on the main trail.

At **1.3 miles**, take a left fork, following the diamonds and arrows. Again, stay on the main trail, through second-growth fir and pine, with rhododendron, salal, and fern for ground cover. After following a creek for a short time, reach a fork. Take either trail as they merge again before crossing a bridge. Cross a paved road at **3 miles**, then cross a dirt road at **3.1 miles**. When the trail forks at **3.2 miles**, turn right, following the Howell Lake Trail. Cross another dirt road at **3.4 miles**, jogging to the left to regain the trail.

Negotiating a corner on the Howell Lake Trail

After paralleling the Tahuya River for a short time, climb a hill and ride parallel to a paved road. The trail crosses the road, Belfair-Tahuya, at **4.6 miles** near a small substation. From here, the trail climbs much of the way back to Howell Lake. At **5.8 miles**, ride straight through a 4-way intersection. Cross several bridges along this stretch. After a particularly steep descent, turn left, away from the road. Just around the corner, **7.1 miles**, reach a 5-way intersection: Take the shallow left. At **7.5 miles**, reach the entrance road, turn left, and ride back to the picnic area to complete the loop, **7.6 miles**.

NOTES:

_____

_____

_____

_____

Ride 58 ⊛

DUVALL TO CARNATION

Distance	**9.0 miles**, one way (18-mile out and back)
Terrain	Wide dirt rail-trail; flat, **no elevation gain**
Duration	1 to 3 hours
Travel	22 miles from Seattle
Skill Level	Beginner
Season	Year round
Map	USGS: *Carnation*
Explorability	Low
Restrictions	None
More Info	King County Parks, 206-296-4298, www.metrokc.gov/parks/

Prelude

This easy, flat rail-trail ride along the Snoqualmie Valley Trail is lovely, crossing through the pasture lands of the lower Snoqualmie Valley between Duvall and Carnation. King County has now extended the trail to Duvall and built a new trailhead there. Watch out when crossing Highway 203 near Carnation.

Driving Directions

Take Highway 520 to Redmond. Cross over Hwy 202, and turn right on Avondale Road. Proceed north. At the Woodinville-Duvall Road, turn right toward Duvall. At Hwy 203 in Duvall, turn left, then immediately turn left again into a parking area next to the bridge.

Spinning through the fields near Duvall

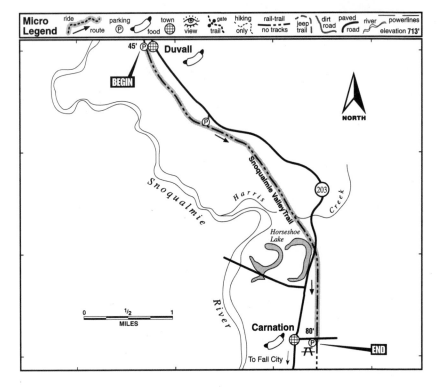

The Ride

Beginning from the parking area, ride south under the bridge along the old railroad grade, which looks like an old road. At **0.2 mile**, pass by McCormick Park. From here, it's flat with long straightaways as you traverse the lowlands of the Snoqualmie River valley. At **2.3 miles**, the trail crosses N.E. 124th Street. At **5.5 miles**, pass a dirt parking area on the left. Pedal across numerous cement bridges. The trail angles across more wide fields.

Whoa—at **7.6 miles**, the trail crosses Hwy 203, so ride with care. Afterwards, the trail bypasses several roads—continue straight ahead. At **9.0 miles**, reach Nick Loutsis Park on the right, the start of the Snoqualmie Valley Trail ride (see Ride 59). If you didn't shuttle a car, turn around and ride 9 miles back to Duvall.

NOTES:

_____

_____

_____

_____

Ride 59 ✹ ✹

SNOQUALMIE VALLEY TRAIL

Distance	**22.4 miles**, out and back
Terrain	Dirt rail-trail, paved roads; flat, **minimal elevation gain**
Duration	2 to 5 hours
Travel	26 miles from Seattle
Skill Level	Beginner
Season	Year round
Maps	USGS: *Carnation*; Green Trails: *Rattlesnake Mountain 205S*
Explorability	Low
Restrictions	None
More Info	King County Parks, 206-296-4298, www.metrokc.gov/parks/

Prelude

The Snoqualmie Valley Trail is an easy ride up the old Milwaukee Railroad grade, through forests and with pleasant views of the valley. This is part of King County's extensive regional trails system, which despite budget constraints is getting improved. Not only has King County already repaired and extended this trail, but they also plan to extend it further north from Duvall to Snohomish County, eventually to meet up with the Centennial Trail. Though the grade is quite easy, the distance may seem intimidating. But there's no reason you can't shorten the ride by turning around before Snoqualmie Falls. For advanced riders, this is a good training ride or winter ride when more sensitive trails are too wet.

Crossing the Tokul Creek Bridge

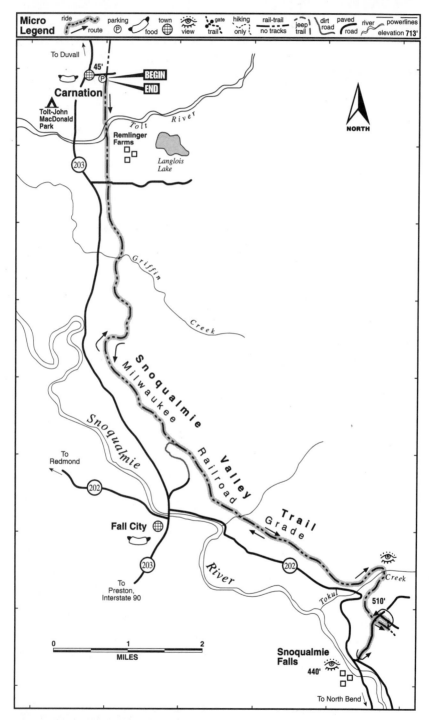

Micro Legend | ride route | parking ⓟ | town food 🌐 | view 👁 | gate trail | hiking only | rail-trail no tracks | jeep trail | dirt road | paved road | river | powerlines | elevation 713'

To Duvall

45'

BEGIN
END

Carnation

Tolt-John MacDonald Park

Remlinger Farms

Tolt River

Langlois Lake

203

NORTH

Griffin Creek

Snoqualmie Valley Trail Grade

Milwaukee Railroad

Snoqualmie

To Redmond

202

Fall City 🌐

203

To Preston, Interstate 90

River

202

Toku Creek

510'

Snoqualmie Falls

440'

To North Bend

0   1   2
MILES

Autumn on the Snoqualmie Valley Trail

Driving Directions

From Seattle, take Highway 520 east to Redmond. Near the end of Hwy 520, turn right onto Highway 202, the Redmond-Fall City Road. Zero out your odometer here, and head east on Hwy 202. At 7.8 miles, turn left on Tolt Hill Road. After a lot of winding, cross the Snoqualmie River, then reach Highway 203 at 11.0 miles. Turn left on Hwy 203. At 11.5 miles, pass Tolt-John MacDonald Park on the right. At 11.8 miles, turn right (east) onto Entwhistle Street. At 12.1 miles, park at the tiny Nick Loutsis Park on the right.

The Ride

From Nick Loutsis Park, find the railroad trail at the back of the parking area and turn right to ride south. After **0.5 mile**, the trail crosses the Tolt River. Pass Remlinger Farms on the left, **0.6 mile**. The way winds easily upward. Ride through several gates and cross a number of roads along the way. Cross a bridge at **4.7 miles**.

At **6.6 miles**, pedal across a high bridge. Cross a road at **6.9 miles**. At **8.6 miles**, Mount Si looms ahead as the trail bends around to the left. At **9.2 miles**, cross a high bridge above Tokul Creek. This is a wonderful place to stop for a moment and take in the views of the valley and the creek far below. At **10.1 miles**, pass through a short tunnel under Tokul Road. Ride about 300 yards farther—on singletrack—then take the trail on the left at a fork, **10.2 miles**, that leads to a paved road. Turn left on the road and ride to the intersection of Tokul Road S.E. and S.E. 60th Street, **10.4 miles**. From here, turn left and ride down Tokul Road to Highway 202, where you'll find the lodge above Snoqualmie Falls, **11.2 miles**. Turn around and retrace your tracks to complete the ride, **22.4 miles**.

NOTES:

Ride 60 ⊗

BOXLEY CREEK

Distance	**10.6 miles**, out and back
Terrain	Wide gravel and dirt rail-trail; flat, **minimal elevation gain**
Duration	1 to 3 hours
Travel	33 miles from Seattle
Skill Level	Beginner
Season	Year round
Map	Green Trails: *Rattlesnake Mountain 205S*
Explorability	Low
Restrictions	None
More Info	King County Parks, 206-296-4298, www.metrokc.gov/parks/

Prelude

Much like other rail-trails, the ride from Tanner, near North Bend, to Rattlesnake Lake offers an easy grade and a wide, compact trail. Add views of Mount Si and the picturesque South Fork of the Snoqualmie River, and it becomes a nice trip. Indeed, this is a great family ride. This trail is an extension of the Snoqualmie Valley Trail and links with Iron Horse State Park at Rattlesnake Lake.

Driving Directions

Drive east on Interstate 90 to Exit 32. At the end of the exit ramp, zero out your odometer, and turn left onto 436th Avenue S.E. At 0.6 mile, turn right on S.E. North Bend Way. At 1.3 miles, bear right at the first paved road (don't pass S.E. Tanner Road), and immediately find the small dirt parking area.

Winter riding on the Snoqualmie Valley Trail near Tanner

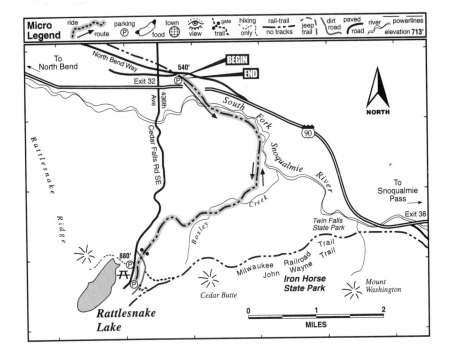

Micro Legend

ride • • • route → parking P • food town ⊕ view ••• gate hiking trail only rail-trail --- no tracks jeep trail dirt road paved road river powerlines elevation 713'

The Ride

The wide gravel trail exits from the back of the small parking area. You'll find the first half-mile the least picturesque as you ride under Interstate 90 and through a gravel playpit for neighborhood BMXers. At **0.4 mile**, though, as soon as the trail crosses a bridge over the South Fork of the Snoqualmie River, the way becomes quite beautiful.

Cross a small residential road at **0.5 mile** and continue up the trail, opposite. After affording some lovely views of the river, the trail bends to the right away from the current, **1.5 miles**. Soon after, cross two deckless bridges over Boxley Creek, the second longer and much higher than the first. After passing around several white gates, reach a gravel road at **4.8 miles**. The trail continues on the opposite side. At **5.3 miles**, reach the parking areas for Rattlesnake Lake, the Rattlesnake Ledge Trail, and Iron Horse State Park (see Ride 61). When you are done picnicking, turn around and return to the parking area at the start of the ride, **10.6 miles**.

NOTES:

Ride 61 ✪✪

IRON HORSE STATE PARK RATTLESNAKE LAKE

Distance	**12.8 miles**, out and back
Terrain	Dirt and gravel rail-trail; slight incline, **cumulative gain: 700 ft.**
Duration	2 to 3 hours
Travel	35 miles from Seattle
Skill Level	Beginner
Season	Year round
Maps	Green Trails: *Rattlesnake Lake 205S, Mount Si NRCA 206S*
Explorability	Low
Restrictions	State Parks vehicle fee, dogs on leash
More Info	Washington State Parks, 360-902-8844, www.parks.wa.gov

Prelude

Several waterfalls cascade down the forested banks above the old Milwaukee Railroad grade, adding sparkle to this ride along the John Wayne Pioneer Trail. Departing from the new Iron Horse State Park trailhead at Rattlesnake Lake, this is an easy rail-trail ride, accessible to any beginner. In the past, the missing Hall Creek trestle forced a rational turnaround point. Since the trestle has now been rebuilt, turning around at Hall Creek is somewhat arbitrary. You can ride all the way to Snoqualmie Pass and beyond (see Rides 62, 63) if you want. The best thing to do is start out from Rattlesnake Lake and see how you feel.

Driving Directions

Drive east on Interstate 90 to Exit 32. At the end of the exit ramp, zero your odometer and turn right onto 436th Avenue S.E., which becomes Cedar Falls Road S.E. Stay on Cedar Falls Road. At 3.3 miles, find Iron Horse State Park's Cedar Falls Trailhead. Park in the paved parking area up to the left.

Following the electric railroad

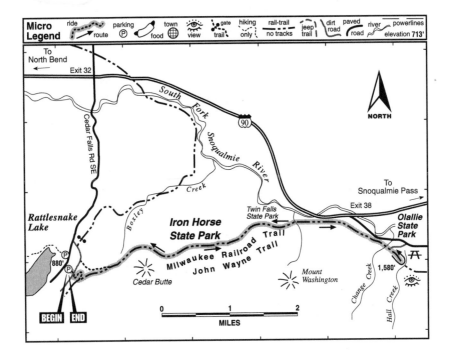

Micro Legend: ride route, parking (P), town/food, view, gate/hiking trail, rail-trail/no tracks, jeep trail, dirt road, paved road, river, powerlines, elevation 713'

To North Bend — Exit 32

South Fork Snoqualmie River

Cedar Falls Rd SE

90

NORTH

To Snoqualmie Pass

Exit 38

Rattlesnake Lake

Boxley Creek

Iron Horse State Park

Milwaukee Railroad Trail
John Wayne Trail

Twin Falls State Park

Olallie State Park

880'

Cedar Butte

Mount Washington

Change Creek

1,580'

Hall Creek

BEGIN END

0   1   2
MILES

The Ride

From the kiosk next to the bathroom, follow the signs for the John Wayne Pioneer Trail. Stay on the wide dirt trail as it climbs gently away from Rattlesnake Lake. At the top of the climb, **0.3 mile**, reach a T and turn left onto the rail-trail, part of the old Milwaukee Railroad grade. From here, the incline is almost imperceptible. Pass by a sign for the Cedar Falls train station, now only a memory.

At **2.0 miles**, cross a short trestle over Boeteke Creek. A delicate waterfall tosses mist into the air on wet days. At **3.3 miles**, cross another trestle with views of a second waterfall on the right. Various roads spur off the main railroad grade—ignore them all. At **4.6 miles**, pass by a small transformer station. At **5.3 miles**, bypass a road that cuts down to the left to Olallie State Park—continue straight on the high road. At **6.1 miles**, cross a long trestle—a beautiful spot to stop for lunch. At **6.3 miles**, cross another trestle. At **6.4 miles**, reach the Hall Creek trestle. Turn around here and retrace your pedal strokes, making the ride **12.8 miles**.

NOTES:

_____

_____

Ride 62 ✹✹✹

IRON HORSE STATE PARK HUMPBACK MOUNTAIN

Distance	**26.8 miles**, out and back
Terrain	Dirt rail-trail; one steep climb then easy, **cumulative gain: 1,200 ft.**
Duration	3 to 5 hours
Travel	39 miles from Seattle
Skill Level	Beginner
Season	Spring, summer, fall
Maps	Green Trails: *Bandera, Snoqualmie Pass*
Explorability	Low
Restrictions	State Parks vehicle fee, dogs on leash
More Info	Washington State Parks, 360-902-8844, www.parks.wa.gov

Prelude

This ride along the abandoned Milwaukee Railroad grade from Olallie State Park to the Snoqualmie Tunnel and back is fairly easy despite the distance and one tough hill near the start. Tracks and ties have been removed from the old railroad grade, a section of the John Wayne Pioneer Trail and part of the Iron Horse State Park system, so the trail is wide, gradual, and mostly smooth. From the trail's perch on slopes above the South Fork of the Snoqualmie River valley, great views abound.

Together along the Milwaukee Railroad grade, a.k.a. John Wayne Pioneer Trail

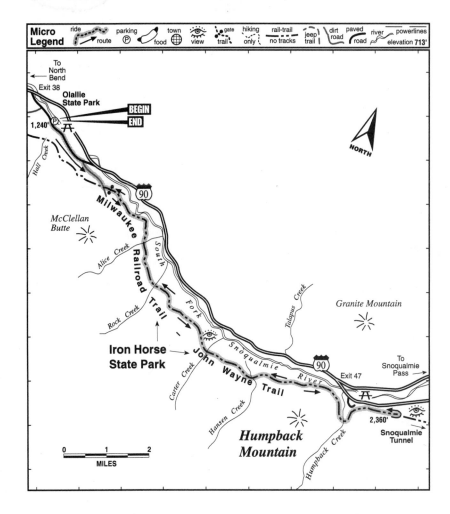

Driving Directions

Drive east on Interstate 90 to Exit 38. Turn right at the bottom of the ramp. Pass an entrance to Olallie State Park on the right. At 0.8 mile, pull into a gravel parking area on the right.

The Ride

From the gravel parking area, continue east on the paved road. When the road divides, **1.1 miles**, turn right onto the dirt road. After a few easy bends, the road heads up, ascending gradually before becoming quite steep. Parts of the final section may require walking. At **2.2 miles**, reach the railroad grade at a 4-way intersection. Turn left, immediately passing through a gate. Pedal up the railroad grade. At **4.2 miles**, pass by the trail to McClellan Butte. At **8.8 miles**, cross a high trestle.

Trestle on the John Wayne Pioneer Trail

As the trail edges around the huge mass of Humpback Mountain (high above on the right), there are many views of the South Fork of the Snoqualmie River. Pass around an old (now gated) avalanche shed at **11.5 miles**. At **11.7 miles**, bypass the trail to Annette Lake and continue up the railroad grade. At **13.4 miles**, reach the entrance to the Snoqualmie Tunnel (see Ride 64). After exploring the tunnel (it's 2.4 miles from end to end), turn around and retrace your tracks back to the parking area near Olallie State Park, **26.8 miles**. The gradual descent on the return trip will increase your speed 5 to 10 miles per hour.

NOTES:

_____

_____

_____

_____

Ride 63 ✾✾✾

IRON HORSE STATE PARK
KEECHELUS LAKE

Distance	**22.8 miles**, one way
Terrain	Dirt and gravel rail-trail, singletrack; easy downhill grade except for 1-mile walk up Annette Lake Trail, **cumulative gain: 800 ft.**
Duration	4 to 7 hours
Travel	48 miles from Seattle
Skill Level	Advanced for first mile, remainder beginner
Season	Summer, fall
Maps	Green Trails: *Snoqualmie Pass*, *Easton*
Explorability	Low
Restrictions	NW Forest Pass, tunnel open May 1 through October 31
More Info	Washington State Parks, 360-902-8844, www.parks.wa.gov

Prelude

The first mile of this ride, providing access to the Iron Horse State Park railroad grade (a.k.a. John Wayne Pioneer Trail) via the Annette Lake Trail, is for the most part completely unridable. However, this route offers a relatively quick way to reach the rail-trail as well as the western entrance to the Snoqualmie Tunnel. And while the rocky and rooted Annette Lake Trail may not exactly be ridable, the deep forest and pleasant gurgle of Humpback Creek make you feel as though it is a good thing to be here, even if you have to push your bike. Be sure to bring a bike light and a wind shell because it's cold and dark in the tunnel. The rest of the ride ambles along the Iron Horse-John Wayne Trail, an easy rail-trail that follows the western edge of Lake Keechelus and the Yakima River. This great "cross-state" trail continues to the Idaho border, though the state parks system is still solidifying the actual route.

Along the Annette Lake Trail

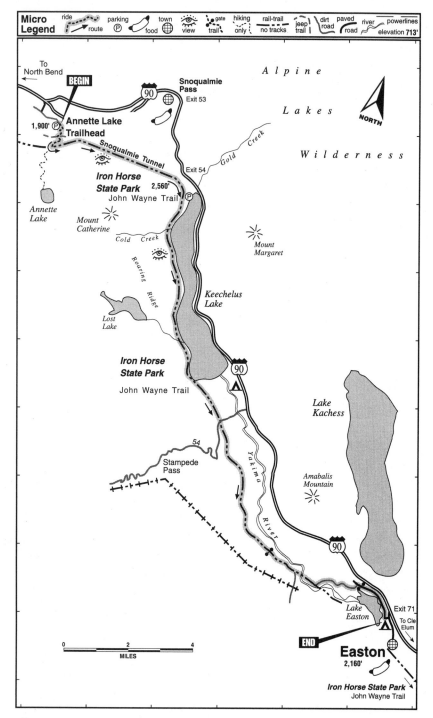

Micro Legend — ride, route, parking ℗, town, food, view, gate, hiking trail, hiking only, rail-trail no tracks, jeep trail, dirt road, paved road, river, powerlines, elevation **713'**

To North Bend

BEGIN

Snoqualmie Pass Exit 53

90

Alpine Lakes Wilderness

NORTH

1,900' ℗ **Annette Lake Trailhead**

Snoqualmie Tunnel

Gold Creek

Exit 54

Iron Horse State Park **2,560'** ℗

John Wayne Trail

Annette Lake

Mount Catherine

Cold Creek

Mount Margaret

Roaring Ridge

Keechelus Lake

Lost Lake

Iron Horse State Park

John Wayne Trail

90

Lake Kachess

54

Stampede Pass

Yakima River

Amabalis Mountain

90

0   2   4
MILES

Lake Easton

Exit 71
To Cle Elum

END

Easton 2,160'

Iron Horse State Park
John Wayne Trail

Into the darkness of the Snoqualmie Tunnel

Driving Directions

From Seattle, take Interstate 90 to Exit 47. At the end of the interstate ramp, set your odometer to zero, and turn right. At 0.1 mile, reach a T and turn left toward the Annette Lake Trailhead. At 0.5 mile, find the trailhead parking lot on the right. Be sure to have a car waiting for you at Lake Easton State Park.

The Ride

From the trailhead, begin the pedal and push up Annette Lake Trail 1019. At **0.25 mile**, cross a bridge over Humpback Creek. At **0.4 mile**, the trail crosses an old road—continue up the trail on the opposite side.

The trail reaches John Wayne Pioneer Trail at **0.9 mile**. Turn left onto the wide, gravel grade. At **2.6 miles**, reach the Snoqualmie Tunnel. From just inside the tunnel's mouth, look for the tiny pinpoint of light at the other end, two and one-half miles away. Emerge from the opposite end of the tunnel at **5.0 miles**. At **5.2 miles**, pass a trailhead on the left, complete with toilets and running water. At **5.8 miles**, pass Iron Horse State Park's Keechelus Lake Trailhead on the left. From here,

Summer riding along Lake Keechelus

the rest of the way is slightly downhill, though occasional stretches of loose gravel keep the speed down. At **6.0 miles**, the trail affords views down to the shores of stump-strewn Keechelus Lake. There's a small picnic area below the trail on the left at **6.3 miles**.

Over the next few miles, the trail parallels the lake. Just after pedaling over a short bridge at **11.8 miles**, pass around a white gate, cross the Moss Lake Road, and continue along the flat, wide railroad grade opposite. At **13.3 miles**, cross the Stampede Pass Road. Ride through a short tunnel at **15.6 miles**. A number of logging roads spur off the trail—stay on the main railroad grade.

At **19.3 miles**, the rail-trail merges with a road—stay to the left. At **19.6 miles**, bear left, following the Iron Horse State Park sign. Cross a bridge. At **20.4 miles**, reach a fork and go left toward Lake Easton State Park. When the trail forks again at **21.2 miles**, bear right. At **21.3 miles**, reach a T at a paved road and turn right. Pass around a gate at **21.6 miles**. There's trailhead parking on the right—a good place for your shuttle vehicle. This is Lake Easton State Park. Pass the campground, then at **22.8 miles**, reach another T. A left turn exits Lake Easton State Park and heads toward I-90 and the town of Easton. A right turn heads toward the lake.

NOTES:

_____

_____

Ride 64 ⊕

IRON HORSE STATE PARK SNOQUALMIE TUNNEL

Distance	**6.4 miles**, out and back
Terrain	Wide gravel rail-trail; flat, **no elevation gain**
Duration	1 hour
Travel	55 miles from Seattle
Skill Level	Beginner
Season	Summer, fall
Map	Green Trails: *Snoqualmie Pass*
Explorability	Low
Restrictions	State Parks vehicle fee, tunnel open May 1 through October 31
More Info	Washington State Parks, 360-902-8844, www.parks.wa.gov

Prelude

Pedaling through the Snoqualmie Tunnel is an easy ride for any cyclist with a bike light (and no phobias of the dark). With two new Iron Horse State Park trailheads, the two-and-a-half-mile tunnel is not only easy but easily accessible. This short, non-technical (yet exciting!) ride is great for adventurous kids with parents in tow. But the tunnel is cold, so be sure to bring along a wind shell and a hat.

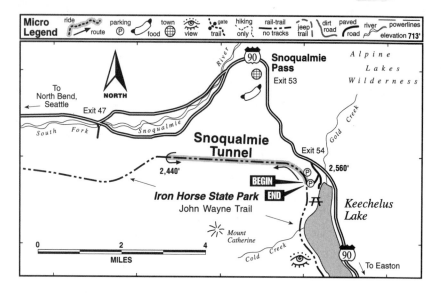

Micro Legend: ride route, parking P, town, food, view, gate, hiking trail, rail-trail no tracks, jeep trail, dirt road, paved road, river, powerlines, elevation 713'

Driving Directions

From Seattle, drive east on Interstate 90 to Exit 54, just past Snoqualmie Summit. At the end of the ramp, zero your odometer and turn right. Immediately turn left, following signs for Iron Horse State Park. At 0.5 mile, turn right. Pass a trailhead on the right, then at 1.0 mile find Keechelus Trailhead on the right.

The Ride

Facing the trail from the parking area, turn right onto the trail, following the signs to the tunnel. At **0.6 mile**, pass by a trail kiosk and trailhead on the right. Just around the corner, **0.8 mile**, reach the entrance to the tunnel.

From the entrance, you should be able to see a pinpoint of light at the western end of the tunnel nearly two and a half miles in the distance. Turn on your light and ride through the dark tunnel. Reach the pinpoint at the opposite end, **3.2 miles**. Retrace your tracks to the parking area to complete the ride, **6.4 miles**.

Option

Pedaling east from the trailhead, you'll find nice views of Keechelus Lake after less than one half-mile. Just before the white gate, find a trail on the left that leads to a pleasant picnic area above the lake.

NOTES:

_____

_____

Ride 65

GRAND RAILROAD TOUR

Distance	**75.3 miles**, one way
Terrain	Dirt and gravel rail-trails, tread loose in places, paved roads; easy grades, **cumulative gain: 2,600 ft.**
Duration	7 to 14 hours
Travel	26 miles from Seattle
Skill Level	Beginner
Season	Summer, fall
Maps	USGS: *Carnation, Fall City*; Green Trails: *Bandera, Snoqualmie Pass, Easton*
Explorability	Moderate
Restrictions	Tunnel open May 1 through October 31
More Info	King County Parks, 206-296-4298, www.metrokc.gov/parks/ Washington State Parks, 360-902-8844, www.parks.wa.gov

Prelude

Imagine riding a bicycle *on dirt* from Carnation over Snoqualmie Pass to Cle Elum. Continue reading—it's not a fantasy (although after you finish, you may wish it was). The Grand Railroad Tour connects five rides and includes the links between them. This trail, most of which is wide, compact, and flat, follows the course of the old Chicago, Milwaukee, Saint Paul and Pacific Railroad, once the longest electric train in the world. In the early 1980s, King County and the State of Washington "rail banked" these corridors when the railroads abandoned them. The tracks and ties are long-gone, and county and state slowly continue to improve

Snow dusting Mount Si

the trail, with new trestles and trailheads. The first 22 miles travel along the Snoqualmie Valley Trail, part of King County's huge regional trails system, between Carnation and Rattlesnake Lake. The remainder of this one-way deathmarch (did I say that?) follows the John Wayne Pioneer Trail, park of Iron Horse State Park. This cacophony of names represents the beginning of the cross-state trail, linking western Washington to Idaho, and ambitious cyclists should it add it to their adventure list. Note: This is a one-way ride, so you have to shuttle a car out to Cle Elum. In addition to a bike light, bring lots of food, liquids, and clothes.

Driving Directions

From Seattle, take Highway 520 east to Redmond. Near the end of Hwy 520, turn right onto Hwy 202, the Redmond-Fall City Road. Zero out your odometer here and head east on Hwy 202. At 7.8 miles, turn left on Tolt Hill Road. After a lot of winding, cross the Snoqualmie River, then reach Hwy 203 at 11.0 miles. Turn left on Hwy 203. At 11.5 miles, pass Tolt-John MacDonald Park on the right. At 11.8 miles, turn right (east) onto Entwhistle Street. At 12.1 miles, park at the tiny Nick Loutsis Park on the right. Remember to leave a car in Cle Elum.

The Ride

From Nick Loutsis Park, turn right onto the rail-trail and ride south. After **0.5 mile**, the trail crosses the Tolt River. The trail crosses a series of trestles, each seemingly higher than the one before. At **9.2 miles**, cross a high trestle above Tokul Creek. At **10.1 miles**, pass through a short tunnel. Ride about 300 yards farther. When the trail splits, turn left—**10.2 miles**—and climb easily to a paved road. Turn left on the road (S.E. 60th Street) and pedal to a T— turn left onto Tokul Road S.E., **10.4 miles**.

At **11.3 miles**, turn left onto S.E. 66th Street. Just down the hill, bear left again onto S.E. Mill Pond Road. The following mile affords excellent views of Mount Si. Reach a T at **12.6 miles** and turn left onto Reinig Road S.E. At **12.9 miles**, find the bridge over the Snoqualmie River. Climb the stairs to the bridge deck and continue riding. Pass the golf course around **13.7 miles**.

The trail passes right beside Mount Si. Cross the river and pass through the east edge of North Bend. Pass Depot Park on the right at **15.5 miles**. After several other road crossings, reach North Bend Way, **17.7 miles**. Carefully cross this road, and find the trail that continues on the opposite side.

Pass through a small gravel parking area, and pedal up the wide rail-trail that exits from the back. Pass under I-90. At **18.1 miles**, the trail crosses a bridge over

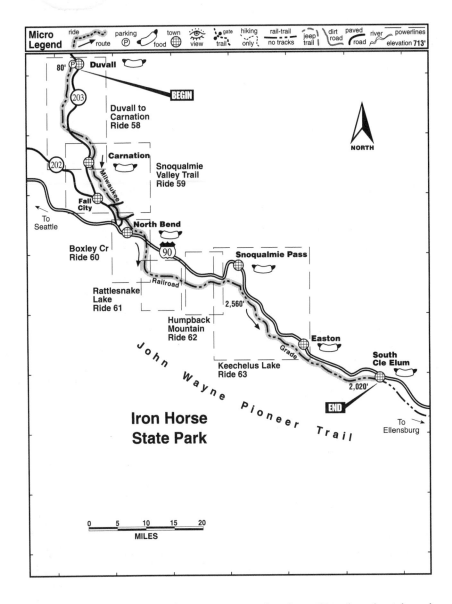

Micro Legend

ride route	parking ℗	town food	view	gate trail
hiking only	rail-trail no tracks	jeep trail	dirt road	paved road
river	powerlines	elevation 713'		

80' ℗ **Duvall**

203

BEGIN

Duvall to Carnation Ride 58

NORTH

202 **Carnation**

Snoqualmie Valley Trail Ride 59

Fall City

To Seattle

North Bend

90

Milwaukee

Boxley Cr Ride 60

Railroad

Snoqualmie Pass

Rattlesnake Lake Ride 61

2,560'

Humpback Mountain Ride 62

Grade

Easton

Keechelus Lake Ride 63

South Cle Elum

2,020'

END

To Ellensburg

J o h n   W a y n e   P i o n e e r   T r a i l

Iron Horse State Park

0	5	10	15	20

MILES

the South Fork of the Snoqualmie River. Soon after, the trail bends to the right and away from the river, **19.2 miles**. The rail-trail crosses a gravel road at **22.4 miles**.

Stay on the main trail as it parallels Cedar Falls Road. At **22.7 miles**, reach the Cedar Falls Trailhead for Iron Horse State Park—it's up to the left. Follow the signs for the John Wayne Pioneer Trail. The wide trail climbs away from the bathrooms, switchbacks gently, then reaches a T at **23.0 miles**. Turn left onto the rail-trail, pedaling up the almost imperceptible grade. At **24.4 miles**, cross a short trestle over Boeteke Creek. Various roads spur off the main railroad grade—ignore them. At **27.0 miles**, pass a small transformer station.

When the trail divides at **27.7 miles**, stay to the right, taking the high road toward the Snoqualmie Tunnel. At **28.8 miles**, cross over Hall Creek trestle. At **30.8 miles**, cross Garcia Road. Pass a picnic area on the left at **33.0 miles**. At **37.4 miles**, cross a high trestle. The trail offers numerous views of the valley to the left. At **40.2 miles**, bypass the trail to Annette Lake, and continue up the railroad grade. At **41.8 miles**, reach the Snoqualmie Tunnel. Pedal through the recently graded, two-and-one-half-mile tunnel, watching the pinpoint of light at the far end grow as you proceed.

Emerge from the opposite end of the tunnel, **44.1 miles**. Pass a large trailhead on the left at **44.3 miles**. At **44.9 miles**, pass the Keechelus Lake Trailhead on the left. From here, the rest of the way is slightly downhill, though occasional stretches of loose gravel keep the speed down. At **45.3 miles**, see views down to the shores of stump-strewn Keechelus Lake. The trail parallels the lake over the next few miles. At **52.3 miles**, cross the Stampede Pass Road. Ride through a short tunnel at **54.7 miles**. A number of logging roads spur off the trail; stay on the main railroad grade.

At **58.7 miles**, the trail merges with a road—stay to the left. At **59.0 miles**, reach a fork and bear left, following the signs toward Iron Horse State Park. Cross over a bridge. When the way forks again at **59.8 miles**, bear left toward Lake Easton State Park. At **60.6 miles**, reach a fork and bear right. Arrive at a T at **60.7 miles** and turn right onto a paved road. Pass a trailhead on the right, then ride alongside the

Snoqualmie Valley Trail near Fall City

Yakima River

campground. At **62.2 miles**, reach a T and turn left to leave Lake Easton State Park. At **62.3 miles**, reach a T and turn right. Descend to the river, then climb easily into the town of Easton. At **63.2 miles**, turn right on Cabin Creek Road. At **63.3 miles**, find the rail-trail crossing Cabin Creek Road at the fire station—turn left onto the trail. From here, the trail is sometimes loose. Whew, it can be hot in the summer.

Cross West Nelson Road and East Nelson Road at **65.8** and **70.0 miles**, respectively. At **70.7 miles**, cross a bridge that spans the Yakima River. After several more road crossings, ride over another Yakima River bridge, **73.0 miles**. After several more miles, the rail-trail parallels a road for a short distance before passing the old Cle Elum Depot Station, at **75.1 miles**. At **75.3 miles**, turn left to exit the Iron Horse Trail at the South Cle Elum Trailhead.

NOTES:

_____

_____

_____

_____

ABOUT THE AUTHOR

In 1980, high school diploma in hand, John Zilly spent nine months circumnavigating the United States on a bicycle, surviving 57 flats over more than 10,500 miles of riding. Several years later, after graduating from Whitman College with a degree in philosophy and touring by bicycle through Europe, he put wide tires on his touring bike and set out to explore the trails of central Idaho. Those explorations developed into *The Mountain Bike Adventure Guide for the Sun Valley Area* (Adventure Press, 1987) and *Son of the Mountain Bike Adventure Guide: Ketchum, Stanley, and Beyond* (Adventure Press, 1992). In 1993 he finished the first edition of *Kissing the Trail: Greater Seattle Mountain Bike Adventures* (Adventure Press). Since then he has published *Wild Pigs: The Mountain Bike Adventure Guide to the Pacific Coast* (Adventure Press, 1995), the second edition of *Kissing the Trail* (Adventure Press, 1997), *Mountain Bike! Northwest Washington* and *Mountain Bike! Southwest Washington* (Sasquatch Books, 1998), *Kissing the Trail: Northwest and Central Oregon Mountain Bike Trails* (Adventure Press, 2000), and *Beyond Mount Si: The Best Hikes within 85 Miles of Seattle* (Adventure Press, 2003). When he's not riding his bike in the mountains, he lives in Seattle.